Up and Running with Autodesk® Inventor® Nastran® 2020

Simulation for Designers

Wasim Younis BEng (Hons), MSc CAE, Cert Ed

DEDICATION

To all the designers and engineers out there who are using Autodesk® Inventor® Nastran® as part of their design process to help them create innovative products.

A SPECIAL THANKS TO JOHN HOLTZ

This edition of the book would not have been possible without the help, guidance and continued support from John Holtz. I am also very grateful to John for allowing me to reuse information produced by him especially around Fatigue in this edition of the book.
Thank you very much John.

 John Holtz is a Technical Support Senior Specialist at Autodesk where he focuses on solving customer's questions related to Autodesk simulation products. Prior to his role in Technical Support, he was a user experience designer and author of the User's Guide, both roles for Simulation Mechanical (Ex Algor). He has a Bachelor of Science degree in mechanical engineering from the University of Pittsburgh and is a professional engineer (P.E.) in the state of Pennsylvania.

COMPUTER AND INVENTOR SETTINGS

This book is using the following settings for screen captures.

Computer settings

Themes

Current theme: Windows

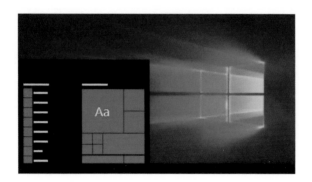

More options

Transparency effects

On

Show the accent colour on the following surfaces

☐ Start, taskbar and action centre

☐ Title bars

Choose your default app mode

◉ Light

◯ Dark

Inventor settings

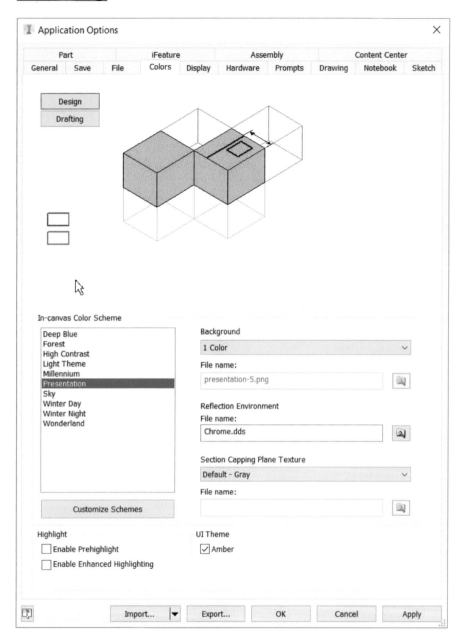

Table of Contents

CONTENTS

Acknowledgements

Foremost, I would like to sincerely thank John Holtz, from Autodesk, for providing me with extensive resources and guidance from whom I continue to learn a great deal. I would also like to extend my thanks to the Inventor Nastran team and my work colleagues Sven Eriksson and Max Edvardsson for their support and suggestions.

My sincere thanks to all the companies, mentioned below, for allowing me to use their datasets, without which none of this would have been possible.

David Scates – Magnet Schultz Limited.
Dennis Fellows – GKN Land Systems.
Jonathan Stancliffe – Canal & River Trust.
Adrian Hartley – Simba Great Plains Ltd.
Graeme Cooper – Howden Compressors.
Kevin Nergaard – Tyne Gangway (Structures) Ltd.
Carl Geldard – Planet Platforms Ltd.

Finally, I would like to thank my wife Samina, daughter Malyah and son's Sami and Fasee for their unconditional love, support and source of inspiration.

Cover image courtesy of Tyne Gangway (Structures) Ltd (www.tynegangway.com).

About the Author

An Autodesk simulation solutions manager with more than 30 years of experience in the manufacturing field, including working at Rolls Royce and British Aerospace. Has been involved with Autodesk simulation software from when it was first introduced, and is well-known throughout the Autodesk simulation community, worldwide.

He has also authored the Up and Running with Autodesk Inventor Professional books including both Inventor FEA and Dynamic Simulation. He also runs a dedicated forum for simulation users on LinkedIn – Up and Running with Autodesk Simulation.

Wasim has a bachelor's degree in mechanical engineering from the University of Bradford and a master's degree in computer- aided-engineering from Staffordshire University.

Currently he is employed @ Symetri (http://www.symetri.com) – an Autodesk value added services partner across UK and Northern Europe.

Contact Details:

Email: younis_wasim@hotmail.com
LinkedIn: https://www.linkedin.com/in/wasimyounis/

Other books published by the author include;

Preface

Welcome to the 2nd edition of *Up and Running with Autodesk® Inventor® Nastran® 2020 – Simulation for Designers.*

Inventor Nastran 2020 is a very capable and comprehensive simulation program which covers a broad spectrum of analysis applications including, linear, thermal, buckling, non-linear and the list goes on.

In this 2nd edition of the book I have included Fatigue Analysis in addition to Linear Stress Analysis. I have also updated content to account for the new features in Inventor Nastran 2020 initial release.

This book has been written using actual design problems, all of which have greatly benefited from the use of simulation technology. For each design problem, I have attempted to explain the process of applying stress analysis using a straightforward, step by step approach, and have supported this approach with explanation and tips. At all times, I have tried to anticipate what questions a designer or development engineer would want to ask whilst he or she were performing the task using Inventor Nastran.

The design problems have been carefully chosen to cover the core aspects and the linear analysis capabilities of Inventor Nastran and their solutions are universal, so you should be able to apply the knowledge quickly to your own design problems with more confidence.

Chapter 1 provides an overview of Inventor Nastran and the user interface and features so that you are well-grounded in core concepts and the software's strengths, limitations and work arounds. Each design problem illustrates a different unique approach and demonstrates different key aspects of the software, making it easier for you to pick and choose which design problem you want to cover first; therefore, having read chapter 1 it is not necessary to follow the rest of the book sequentially.

In this edition I have included three new chapters focusing around Fatigue Analysis. Chapter 11 provides an overview of Fatigue, including a hand calculation, and Chapter 12-13 go through step by step guidance on how to perform Multi-Axial Fatigue analysis within Inventor Nastran.

This book is primarily designed for self-paced learning by individuals but can also be used in an instructor-led classroom environment.

I hope you will find this book enjoyable and at the same time very beneficial to you and your business. I will be very pleased to receive your feedback, to help me improve future editions. Feel free to email me on ***younis_wasim@hotmail.com***

How to access training files

All files necessary to complete the exercises can be accessed from;

http://vrblog.info/

The Book exercises are available on the bottom of the blog page (available on all pages/posts). You may need to scroll-down a little to see the exercise-files available via Box.net

Alternative links to download exercises for this edition of the book.

https://tinyurl.com/yycrpvkl
https://tinyurl.com/y2nd8ca5

The Inventor Nastran Environment

The Finite Element Method (FEM) - An Overview

The finite element method (FEM) is a mathematical/computer-based numerical technique for calculating the strength and behaviour of engineering structures. Autodesk Nastran In-CAD – and much other analysis software – are based on the FEM, where simply a component is broken down into many small elements, as shown below.

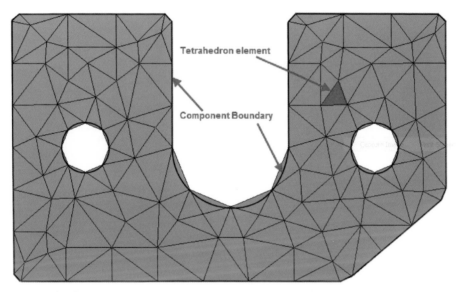

Discretization of a component into a number of Tetrahedron finite elements

Let's assume that we need to determine the displacement of the component. This displacement (unknown quantity) acts over each element in a predefined manner – with the number and type of elements chosen so that overall distribution through the component is sufficiently approximated. This distribution across each element is commonly presented by a polynomial – whether it's linear, quadratic or even cubic. It is important to note FEM is always an approximation of the actual component and by its very nature will have errors due to discretization - particularly around curved boundaries (as shown above) or geometrically complex components.

These errors due to discretization can be reduced by either specifying more elements or using higher order polynomials to approximate the distribution of the unknown quantity over the elements - also referred to as polynomial interpolation function. Most finite element software uses the former method, specifically known as the H refinement process, in which the software goes through an iterative process of increasing the number of elements at each iteration until the results have converged. The latter method, of using higher order polynomials, is called the P-refinement process, in which the software increases the order of the polynomial at each iteration starting from 1(linear) to 2(quadratic), 3(cubic) and so on.

Types of Finite Element Method (FEM) Elements

Autodesk Nastran In-CAD uses the following elements.

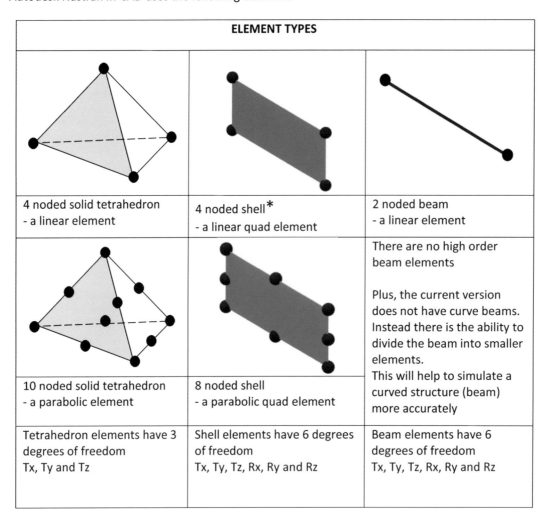

ELEMENT TYPES		
4 noded solid tetrahedron - a linear element	4 noded shell* - a linear quad element	2 noded beam - a linear element
10 noded solid tetrahedron - a parabolic element	8 noded shell - a parabolic quad element	There are no high order beam elements Plus, the current version does not have curve beams. Instead there is the ability to divide the beam into smaller elements. This will help to simulate a curved structure (beam) more accurately
Tetrahedron elements have 3 degrees of freedom Tx, Ty and Tz	Shell elements have 6 degrees of freedom Tx, Ty, Tz, Rx, Ry and Rz	Beam elements have 6 degrees of freedom Tx, Ty, Tz, Rx, Ry and Rz

* Inventor Nastran also provides the option of a 3 noded (linear) and 6 noded (parabolic) triangular shell elements.

The following tube example will be used to demonstrate the results obtained by using different element types.

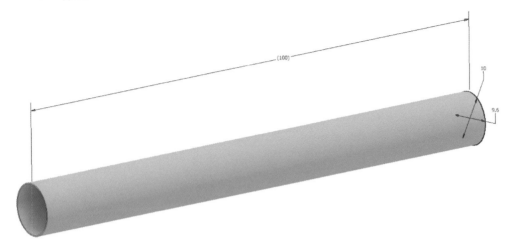

Initially we will determine the theoretical results for a simply supported tube using the following data.

Length = 100mm
OD = 10mm
Thickness = 0.2mm
Material = Mild Steel
Load = 100N

Using the classical Bending Stress Equation:

$$\frac{M}{I} = \frac{\sigma}{y} = \frac{E}{R}$$

We can determine the maximum moment of the tube at the centre.

$Mmax$ = Length x Load/4 = 100 x 100/4 = 2,500Nmm

y = 5mm

$I = \pi/64 \ (\emptyset_{outside}^4 - \emptyset_{inside}^4) = \pi/64 \ (10^4 - 9.6^4) = 73.95mm^4$

$$\sigma max = \frac{My}{I} = \frac{2500 \ x \ 5}{74.18} = 169MPa$$

Stress Analysis Results - using 10 noded tetrahedron elements – 157.7N/mm^2 or (157.7MPa)

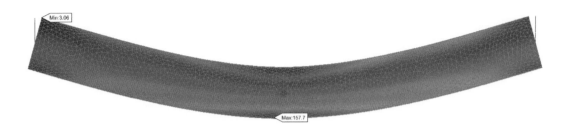

% difference = 6.69% based on using von mises stress (centroidal based) and max element size of 1, for comparison purposes. This value is acceptable as it is within 10% of theoretical value, based on best practices.

Stress Analysis Results - using 8 noded quad shell elements – 172.8N/mm^2

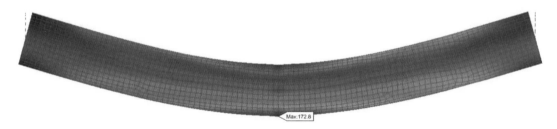

% difference = 2.25% based on using von mises stress (centroidal based) and max element size of 1, for comparison purposes. This indicates that shell elements yield better results than solid elements for thin structures, with the added advantage of having a lot less elements.

Stress Analysis Results - using 2 noded beam elements – 171 N/mm^2

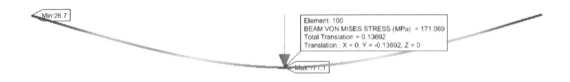

% difference = 1.3% based on using von mises stress and max element size of 1, for comparison purposes. This further suggests beam elements yield better results for structures with uniform cross section.

 Use beam elements for structures with a uniform cross section that also have a length to cross section ratio above 30.

Static analysis - an overview

Static analysis is an engineering discipline that determines the stress in materials and structures subjected to static or dynamic forces or loads. The aim of the analysis is usually to determine whether the element or collection of elements, usually referred to as a structure or component, can safely withstand the specified forces and loads. This is achieved when the determined stress from the applied force(s) is less than the yield strength of the material. This stress relationship is commonly referred to as factor of safety (FOS) and is used in many analyses as an indicator of success or failure in analysis.

$$\textbf{Factor of Safety} \; = \; \frac{\text{Yield Stress}}{\text{Calculated Stress}} = \frac{\text{Ultimate Stress}}{\text{Calculated Stress}}$$

Factor of Safety can be based on either Yield or Ultimate stress limit of the material. The factor of safety on yield strength is to prevent detrimental deformations and the factor of safety on ultimate strength aims to prevent collapse.

Below are some examples of where static analysis can be useful.

Canal Bridge

The canal bridge is a typical example of static analysis. Here, one will be interested to know whether the bridge will withstand a load of a vehicle when it crosses the bridge. This will help to identify weak parts of the structure, ultimately allowing us to design a bridge to carry the maximum physically possible load.

In another example one might be interested in the maximum deflection of the fan blade, which can have an impact on the efficiency of the fan. With the help of static analysis, the blade can be studied and analysed to reduce deformation, for example by using different materials, increasing the thickness, or adding structural stiffeners.

One of the major obstacles when conducting static analyses is stress singularities, which can significantly distort results and can reduce confidence in the results, as illustrated and discussed in the next section.

Stress singularities

Stress Singularities are a major concern when analysing results as they considerably distort results. They are also a main cause for non-convergence of results. So, the first question - what is stress singularity? This can be best explained by the following example.

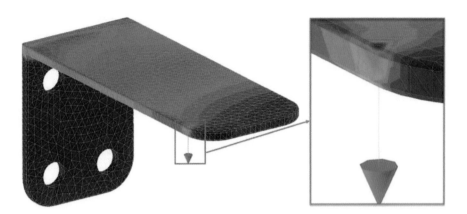

This bracket has a high localised stress around the force applied on a point. This stress can be considerably higher than the operational stress and applying a denser mesh around this simply leads to a much higher stress. This phenomenon is known as stress singularity where the stress can become infinite, as illustrated by the following formula:

$$\textbf{Stress (infinite)} = \frac{\text{Force}}{\text{Area of point (almost} = 0)}$$

Therefore, to avoid stress singularities when applying loads, it is recommended **not to apply loads at points and small edges**.

Stress Singularities can also occur **by applying constraints on points and small edges** – even faces with sharp corners as illustrated below.

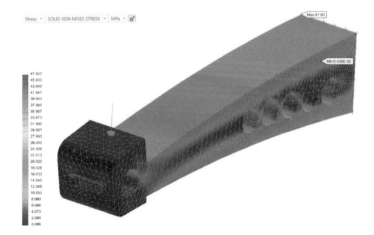

In the above example, stress singularities resulted from using a finer mesh, whereas the image on next page of the same model is showing max stress in a different location as a result of using a coarser mesh. Therefore, interpret results with care.

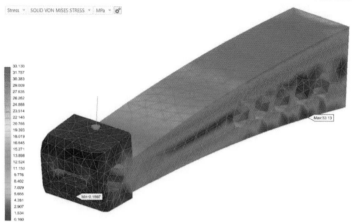

💡 Gain further confidence in your results by using mesh convergence, mentioned later in this chapter, where models have stress singularities present.

Finally, another cause of stress singularity *is over-simplification of components*. Let's look at the following example.

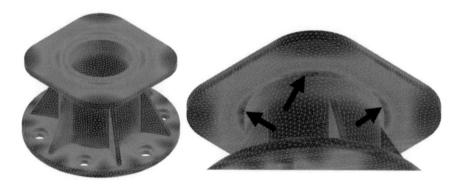

In this example, the fillets have been removed to simplify the analysis; however, when we keep refining the mesh, the maximum stress value does not converge as all the stress is concentrated around the edge, as shown above. In this scenario it would be advisable to un-suppress the fillets to help distribute the load more uniformly as shown below.

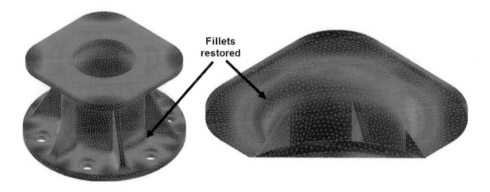

Fillets restored

So, in brief to avoid stress singularities within models do:

1. Avoid applying loads on points and small edges.
2. Avoid restraining faces with sharp corners, including points and small edges.
3. Apply fillets and chamfers to evenly distribute loads.

Stress Analysis Workflow

The process of creating a stress analysis study involves four core steps:

Step 1 — IDEALIZATION – Use solid, shell or beam elements or combination of either. Including simplifying geometry.

Step 2 — BOUNDARY CONDITIONS – Apply constraints and loads, including materials, contacts, connector and mesh setup.

Step 3 — RUN SIMULATION AND ANALYSE – Analyse initial results, including convergence of results using mesh sensitivity study.

Step 4 — REDESIGN – Modify geometry to meet design goals, including changing original materials.

Inventor Nastran User Interface

Inventor Nastran can be accessed from both the Part and Assembly environment via the Environments tab.

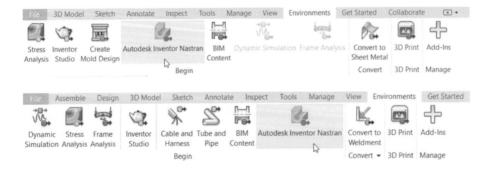

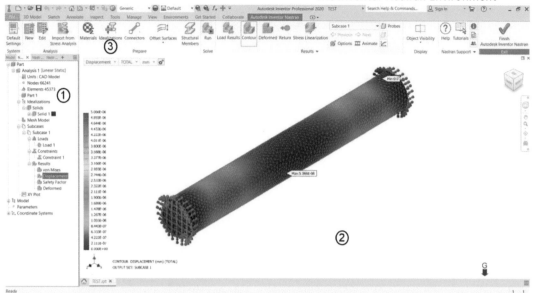

1. Inventor Nastran browser.
2. Inventor Nastran graphic window.
3. Inventor Nastran Panel.

Inventor Nastran browser

Displays the analysis with part or assembly information in a hierarchical view with nested levels of feature and attribute information. The browser information is mainly split into four sections.

1. Analysis Information.
2. Model information.
3. Parameters.
4. Coordinate systems.

Analysis information

When entering the Inventor Nastran environment for the first time every analysis is named Analysis 1 and Linear Static analysis being set as the default analysis type. Multiple analysis and types can exist in the browser. Analysis section is the primary location for defining the analysis. The information available is dependent on the active analysis type. However, the following information are standard for the default Analysis 1.

FE Model

1. Mesh Model – Contains the mesh settings for the analysis.
2. Physical Properties – Contains information whether the geometry is represented by either solid, shell or line elements including material information.

Subcases

1. Constraints – Includes info on how geometry is constrained.
2. Loads – Includes how geometry is loaded to represent real life.

 Duplicate subcases to investigate geometry under different loading conditions.

You need to duplicate analysis to compare effects of different mesh settings.

Results

Once the analysis run has completed the results information becomes available. The information depends on what was requested by the analysis options. Results can be accessed by double clicking on any one of the default result plots. Comprehensive tools are also available to extract specific types of information including, animate, section views, elemental results and more by right clicking and selecting edit on any one of the default result plots.

Model information

Contains all the information from the analysis including the following.

Materials – Contains a list of materials that have been added to the model. You can also create new material from here for further analysis.

Physical properties – Contains list of physical properties that have been added to the model. You can also create new physical properties from here for further analysis.

Composite Layups – Contains the list of composite layups that have been added. Also enables you to create new laminates and global plies for association with the shell property for composite analyses.

Constraints – Contains list of constraints that have been added to the model. You can also create new constraints from here for further analysis.

Loads – Contains the list of loads that have been added to the model with the ability to create more from here.

Concentrated Masses – Contains the list of concentrated masses that are being used in the analyses to represent complex geometry. The first concentrated mass can only be created from here. Additional masses can be created from both model and analysis information tree.

Connectors – Contains the list of connectors that have been added to the model. You can also create new connectors from here for further analysis

Dampings – Contains the list of damping instances that have been added to the model and enables the creation of new ones.

Tables – Contains the list of tables that have been added to the model. You can also create new ones from here.

Surface Contacts – Contains the list of automatic or manual contacts that have been added to the model. You can also create new contacts from here for further analysis.

Plot Templates – Contains specified results views that can be used to report on an analysis and enables you to create new ones.

Groups – Contains list of Node and Element groups used in contact definition and XY plotting.

 You can drag and drop settings from the model section to the analysis section within the browser.

 You can only delete settings from the model section.

Parameters

Inventor Nastran has over hundreds off parameters that can be accessed to control Inventor Nastran. Typically, most parameters will be specified via the user interface, but you also have the option to access them from here for more advanced and direct control.

Coordinate Systems

Contains a list of the current coordinate systems that have been transferred from the inventor environment. You can also create and define new coordinate systems from here based on cylindrical, spherical and cartesian coordinates.

Inventor Nastran graphic window

Display's the model geometry and analysis results. Updates to show the current status of the analysis including boundary conditions and loads. Geometry can be manipulated using view cube, navigation bar and marking menu (heads-up-display) and more. Once the results are loaded you can very easily display different results using the results navigation bar as shown below.

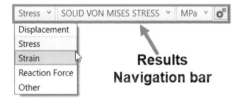

Inventor Nastran file formats

Inventor Nastran creates the following additional files in the same location from where the CAD model was accessed.

.NAS – This file contains a complete description of the bulk data that was used to define the model. It contains data including model geometry, elements, nodes and loads.

.LOG – This file contains the analysis data and information on what is happening in the solver as the process progresses through the run.

.FNO – This binary file contains the post processed results. This is the file which contains information used for displaying results.

.OUT – This ASCII file contains the information that is displayed in the browser. It summarizes the mass matrix, element results, warnings and errors.

.RSF – This file provides a concise list of analysis results. The element results, warning and errors are not included.

Inventor Nastran Panel

Panel buttons	Workflow stage	Description
Default Settings		**Default Settings –** Allows you to select some settings for Inventor Nastran User-Interface, including the ability to set units.
New Edit		**New (Edit) Analysis –** Here you can select (or modify) the type of analysis you want to create and analyse, including result options you desire.
Import from Stress Analysis		**Import Analysis –** Allows you to transfer boundary conditions from inventor stress analysis environment.
Idealizations		**Idealization –** Here you can simplify the representation of your model using solid, shell or line elements.
Materials		**Materials –** Allows you to select and modify materials.
Connectors	**Step 1**	**Connectors –** Create special line elements including bolt and rigid connections.
Offset Surfaces		**Surfaces –** Create surfaces automatically or manually to represent thin parts.
Structural Members		**Structural Members –** Here you can select which members you would like to represent as beams or solids.
Constraints		**Constraints –** Define how models are constrained to represent reality as closely as possible.
Loads	**Step 2**	**Loads –** Here you can define loads that are exerted on a component in the real world.
Auto Manual Solver		**Contacts –** Create contacts between components automatically or manually.
Mesh Settings Table Generate Mesh Mesh Control		**Mesh –** Preview and create mesh, including global and local mesh refinement.

Inventor Nastran Panel continued

Panel buttons	Workflow stage	Description
Run		**Run** – Click to generate results.
Load Results		**Load Results** – Select this to populate previously generated results.
Contour		**Contour** – View results to help make an informed decision on whether the component will function.
Deformed		**Deformed** – Select to see how the component will deform.
Return		**Return** – Select to switch between post-processing and pre-processing environment.
Stress Linearization	Step 3	**Stress Linearization** – Utility to graph specified stress tensors along a Stress Classification Line.
Subcase 1 - Copy / Previous / Next / Options / Animate		**Options (Animate)** – Select to display different subcase results and to modify result settings.
Probes		**Probes** – Select to create probes at areas of interest. Also, can now display convergence plot.
Object Visibility		**Object Visibility** – Allows you to hide and unhide objects including, mesh, loads, constraints etc.
Help Tutorials		**Nastran Support** – Provides numerous supports to get you up and running with Inventor Nastran.

Default Settings

Default
Settings

Allows you to select some settings for the Inventor Nastran User-Interface.

General

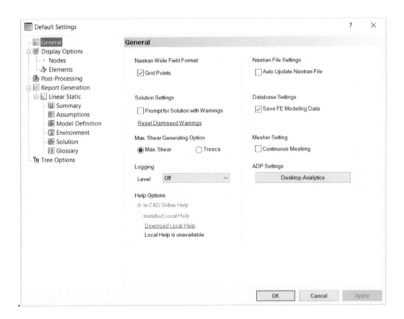

Nastran Wide Field Format – When checked grid points are displayed in wide field format within the Nastran File window.

Nastran File Settings – When checked the .NAS file is continuously updated. This setting is primarily needed for running Nastran solutions from the Nastran File window.

Solution Settings – When checked Inventor Nastran will prompt the user if it should continue when the solver encounters any warnings and errors. An example could be a missing load in a linear analysis and if checked the solver will continue.

Database Settings – This is in my opinion the most useful setting here. When checked all the analysis settings will be saved within inventor file.

Uncheck database settings to quickly remove all Nastran information when your re-open file.

Max Shear Generating Option – The user can select between Max Shear or Tresca failure criterion.

Mesher Setting – This option only applies to surface meshing. When continuous meshing is selected it will force all the adjacent element nodes to be merged and connected.

Logging – Should always be off unless sending a support case to Autodesk. Again, this optional.

ADP Settings – Here you have the option to remove yourselves from Autodesk analytics programs.

Further details can be obtained from the on-line help.

Display Options

Display – Here the user can set global visualisation of boundary conditions including constraints, loads, concentrated mass, connectors, free edges, mesh control and more.

Rendering – When checked will optimize the graphics for fast rendering.

Undeformed Edge Display – When checked will display undeformed edges when deformed plot is displayed.

Nodes

This controls visibility of the nodes in the model, including the ability to change size and colour of nodes. Users can choose to display nodes with either the displacement coordinate system or id tag.

Elements

This controls the visibility of labels in the model, including the ability to display elements in the model by id, material, or property.

Post-Processing

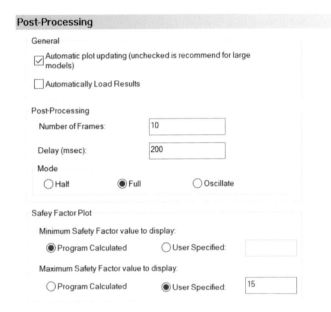

General

Is associated with loading of results.

Automatic plot updating – Selected by default and displays default results automatically once run has completed. Recommended to be unchecked for large models.

Automatically Load Results – Suggest having it unchecked always. You can load results if you need to see them again.

Post-Processing

Is associated with animations and the following attributes can be defined.

Number of Frames – Here you can define the number of frames. Generally higher numbers yield smoother animations.

Delay (msec) – This time is associated between animation frames.

Mode – This controls how the animation is displayed.

Half - Animation starts at the unloaded/undeformed state and gradually advances to the fully loaded/deformed results and stops.

Full - The first half is same as Half mode and then reverses gradually returning to the unloaded/undeformed state.

Oscillate - The first half of the animation is identical to the Full mode. Then, a second full-cycle is added using a mirror image of the calculated deformed shape.

Safety Factor Plot

Is associated with setting minimum and maximum values for safety factor plots.

Minimum Safety Factor value to display – Here you can set a minimum value for plots rather than program calculated value.

Maximum Safety Factor value to display – Here you can set a maximum value for plots rather than program calculated value.

Report Generation

Here you can define a custom unit other than the default units for the report in addition to being able to customise the text written to the report.

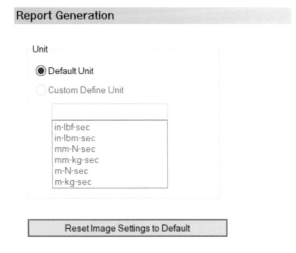

 Currently reports can only be generated for Linear Static solutions.

Tree Options

Here you can hide (untick) information under the model section in the browser including materials, idealizations etc. You also have the option to hide (untick) nodes and elements which appear in analysis section and display total number of nodes and elements.

The default settings window can also be accessed by right-clicking anywhere in the browser and selecting default settings.

New (Edit) Analysis

New   Edit

Linear Static is the default analysis type when you first enter the Inventor Nastran environment with a new part or assembly.

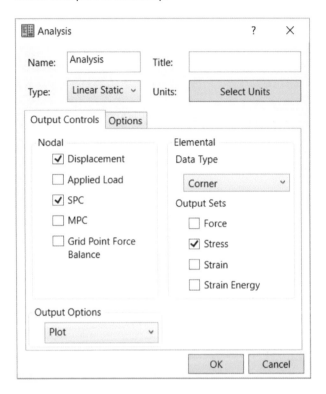

Name – Here you can specify a suitable name for the analysis.

Title – Allows you to enter additional comments about the analysis.

Type – Here you can choose the type of analysis you desire from a comprehensive list.

This edition of the book will focus only on Linear Static and Multi Axial Fatigue analyses.

Units – This allows you to select a unit system for the analysis other than the default CAD units.

Nodal – This section allows you select what nodal data is required for results post-processing. For example, SPC data is needed to determine the reaction loads at constraint locations.

Elemental – This section is split into two areas. The first allows you select whether the results displayed are elemental or nodal (corner) based. Secondly you can select what elemental data is required for results post-processing. For example, force data is needed to determine forces in beam elements.

Output Options – This controls the results output file options. In most cases you do not need to change this.

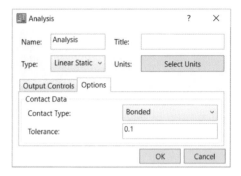

Contact Type – This allows you to select which contact option you would like to generate when the automatic contact generation button is used.

Tolerance – This allows you to generate automatic contacts between components which are within the specified tolerance.

Import from Stress Analysis

Import from
Stress Analysis

Selecting the Import from Stress Analysis button will create a new linear static analysis. The subcases will be automatically populated with loads and constraints that were defined in Inventor Stress Analysis.

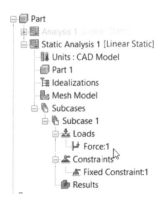

Idealizations and mesh settings will not be imported from Inventor Stress Analysis.

Materials

Materials

Typically, the linear material properties will be assigned automatically within the Nastran environment.

Select Material – Here you can select materials from the usual Inventor and Autodesk material library that come with Inventor. In addition, Inventor Nastran allows you to select materials from the Nastran library.

Type – Here you can select the material behaviour of the component from the list available.

Idealization – Lists the idealizations available in the file, to which the materials can be assigned.

Save New Material – This allows you to create your own custom materials to be used later.

Analysis Specific Data – These are further properties that need to be defined for specific analysis types. Nonlinear and PPFA analyses are not covered in this edition of the book. Please refer to online help for further information.

 Linear analysis only requires density, poison ratio and young's modulus to generate accurate results.

 Allowables are only needed for Safety Factor plots. Alternatively, you can calculate manually.

Idealizations

Idealizations

Inventor Nastran allows to represent geometry using any of the following idealizations;

1. Solid.
2. Shell.
3. Line.

By default, a solid idealization is created which can be modified.

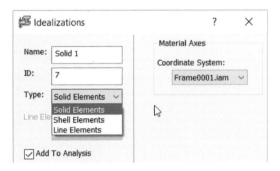

Name – Suggesting an appropriate name for an idealization is helpful especially when there are many idealizations.

ID – This field is automatically populated by Nastran.

Add To Analysis – Is checked by default and will add the idealization to the analysis in addition to the model tree.

Solid

Material is only required to fully define a solid idealization.

Associated Geometry – If selected will allow you to select individual components otherwise the idealization will be applied to all components.

Shell

To fully define a shell idealization both material and thickness are required.

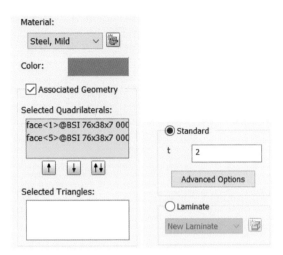

Inaddition shell elements allows you to select either Quadrilateral or Triangular elements. By default quadrilaterals are selected. Use the vertical arrow buttons to move selected items from one list to the other, or to swap the contents of the two boxes.

Advanced Options – Allows you to specify more parameters to control your shell elements.

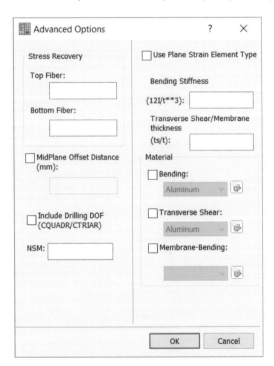

Stress Recovery - Top and Bottom Fiber allows you to see the bending stress from a different location. If left blank the bending stress will be from the surface of the plate (1/2 the thickness from the neutral axis). An example where you may want to specify values here is perhaps to take account for any insulation or coating on a plate that adds to the thickness but not the stiffness. This value will not affect displacement results.

MidPlane Offset Distance (mm) – Allows you specify a value when the mesh is not located at the mid-thickness. For example, let's take the example below which shows a surface model of a tank with a nozzle and reinforcing pad around the nozzle.

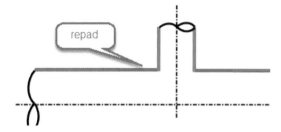

By default, the input indicates that the shells are arranged like this:

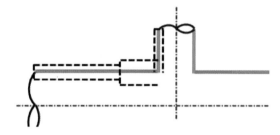

In reality, the plates are arranged like this. Note how the mid-thickness are not inline:

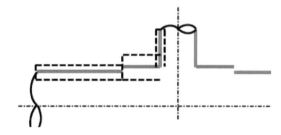

You can use the "MidPlane Offset Distance" offset to simulate the above arrangement.

Include Drilling DOF – Activate when you want to transfer moments whose direction is perpendicular to the plane of the shell. Otherwise, moment loads in the out-of-plane direction are not calculated.

NSM – (Non-Structural Mass) Allows you to specify a value. An example could be when there is insulation applied to the face of the shell or some other uniform mass that is not included in the mass density.

Laminate – Allows you to define a composite laminate property. Composite Analysis is not covered in this edition of the book.

Refer to online help for further information.

Line

Inventor Nastran offers the following line elements.

1. **Bar –** Allows for loads to be transmitted in all degrees of freedom. This is the most commonly used line element within Inventor Nastran.
2. **Beam –** In addition to bar elements allows you to specify sectional properties at either end of a tapered line element. Also, allows you to define additional L section properties.
3. **Pipe –** Allows you to specify internal pipe pressure.

Bar Element

To fully define Bar idealization both material and cross section properties of the beam are required. Cross sectional properties of the bar can be defined by either one of the following.

1. Property Input
2. Cross Section
3. Structural Member

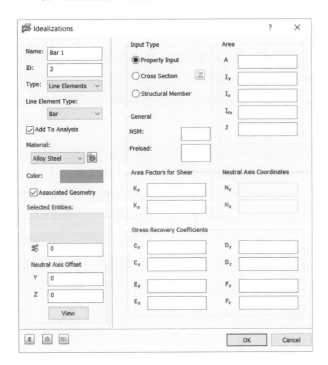

 – Here you can rotate the section so that proper orientation of the section is obtained.

Neutral Axis Offset

Y – This allows the section to be offset in the elemental Y direction.

Z – This allows the section to be offset in the elemental Z direction.

View - Shows the neutral coordinate system of the selected line. The X-axis is from End A to End B of the line element and the Y-axis is the vertical direction in the cross section.

 The Display Coordinate System option must be allowed to be able to view this feature.

Property Input

NSM   – A non-structural mass for the line elements will be used in calculations.

Preload – Defines an axial preload value (not for use in nonlinear solutions).

Area   – Cross section area.

Iz   – Moment of inertia about Z neutral axis.

Iy   – Moment of inertia about Y neutral axis.

Izy   – Product of inertia.

J   – Torsional Constant.

Kz   – Shear factor in Z.

Ky   – Shear factor in Y.

Nz   – Centroid offset from shear centre in Z (appears only for Beam type).

Ny   – Centroid offset from shear centre in Y (appears only for Beam type).

Cz   – Z coordinate of stress recovery point C.

Cy   – Y coordinate of stress recovery point C.

Dz   – Z coordinate of stress recovery point D.

Dy   – Y coordinate of stress recovery point D.

Ez   – Z coordinate of stress recovery point E.

Ey   – Y coordinate of stress recovery point E.

Fz   – Z coordinate of stress recovery point F.

Fy   – Y coordinate of stress recovery point F

In most cases you only need to define A, Iy, Iz, Izy and J properties.

Cross Section

This option allows you to specify sizes of cross section based on standard shapes.

In additions to cross sectional properties the following optional properties can also be specified.

NSM – Defines non-structural mass.

Preload – Specify a preload value.

Offset To – These options refer to the actual mesh (numerical representation) of the model.

Centroid – Will mesh to the centroid of the library part used.

Shear Center – Will mesh the selected structural members to the offset shear centre.

Reference Point – Can be assigned to a location on the cross-section and then the section offset to this reference point location.

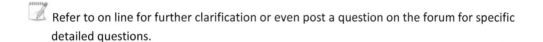 Refer to on line for further clarification or even post a question on the forum for specific detailed questions.

– Clicking this icon brings up the Cross Section Definition window.

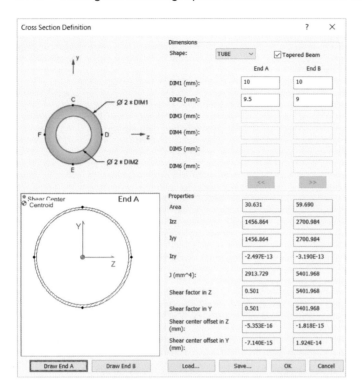

Shape – You can select standard cross-sectional shapes from the drop-down list (T, I, etc.).

DIM1, DIM2 – Depending on the shape selected number of DIM values become available for you to enter values to represent geometry.

Draw End A (Draw End B) – Once the cross-section dimensions are filled in, these buttons are pressed to view the shape and to populate the properties.

Tapered Beam – This option is available only for beam elements as shown above in the Cross Section Definition dialogue box.

>> – Buttons will become active when **Offset To** option is set to **Reference Point**. This will activate a reference point that can be moved around the cross section as an offset location for a beam. This is generally used with stiffening panels.

Structural Member

This option is selected by default and will automatically create beam idealizations with all the necessary data, if structures have been created using frame generator.

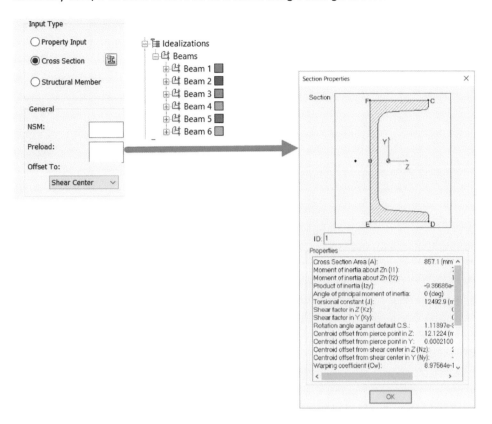

Using structural member options will create individual idealizations for each individual structure, even with the same cross section, resulting in excessive idealizations.

Cross section option can significantly reduce number of idealizations required for structures with same cross section size.

Connectors

Connectors

In this current release of Inventor Nastran you can define the following connectors.

1. Rod.
2. Cable.
3. Spring.
4. Rigid Body.
5. Bolt.

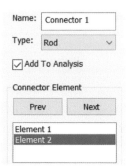

Connector Element – Allows to create multiple connectors with the same name.

All connectors, except Rigid Body and Bolt, are created by selecting two endpoints. Depending on the type of connector chosen further properties need to be specified to fully define the connectors.

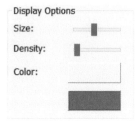

Size, density and colour of connector symbols can be modified for all connectors

Rod

The following properties need to be further specified for Rod connectors.

A – Cross sectional area of rod.

J – Polar Moment of Inertia.

C – Stress Recovery Location.

NSM – Non-Structural Mass.

Cable

The following properties need to be further specified for Cable connectors.

U_o – Initial Cable Slack.

T_o – Initial Tension.

A – Cross sectional.

I – Moment of Inertia.

S_T – Allowable Tensile Stress.

PreLoad:

Initial – Informs solver T_o is initial preload of cable.

Continuous – Informs solver T_o is actual preload of cable & remains constant.

Spring

The following properties need to be further specified for Spring connectors.

GE – Defines the elemental Damping Coefficient to be used if elemental damping is used in a dynamic analysis.

Grounded Spring – Select this for a spring connector that is attached to a single endpoint.

Stiffness – Allows you to define stiffness of the spring.

Advanced options
Allow you to specify different stiffness and damping values in all degrees of freedom. Directions are in the default part coordinate system unless specified otherwise. 123 corresponds to the translational degrees of freedom and 456 corresponds to rotational degrees of freedom.

Stress/Strain recovery coefficients within advance options are used as stress and strain recovery if the value is different from a unit value. Typically, these are never changed.

Refer to online help for further clarification.

Rigid Body

The following properties need to be further specified for Rigid connectors.

To fully define a connector, you need to select dependent entities and a point. The point can be automatically created, using Point At Center, or by selecting an existing 3D work point or sketch point. By default, all six degrees of freedom for the rigid connector are selected. This means that there is no relative motion between the point and dependent entities. You can uncheck some of the degrees of freedom if there is relative motion. There are two types of rigid bodies

1. Rigid Body.
2. Interpolation.

Choose the type carefully as the results can be completely different, as demonstrated in the following example.

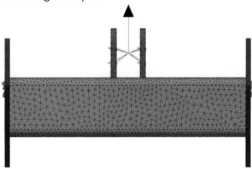

Rigid Body

Using this type of connector creates an infinitely stiff connection, which can also add additional stiffness to the model.

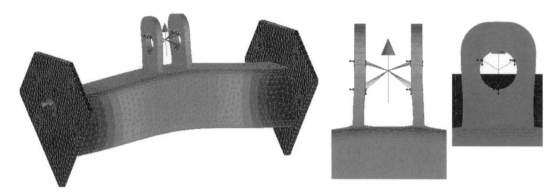

In example above, you can see there is no relative displacement between the two lug components including no hole deformation.

Interpolation

This type of connector does not create an infinitely stiff connection and instead uses weighted averages of the nodes to determine the displacement.

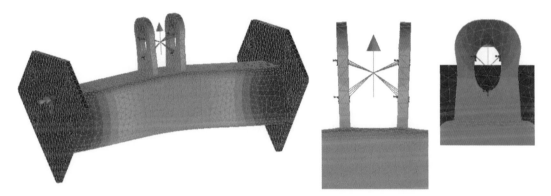

In example above, you can see there is some relative displacement between the two lug components including some hole deformation.

📝 Deformation is not actual.

📝 Take care interpreting rigid connector results.

Bolt

The following properties need to be further specified for Bolt connectors.

Bolt

To define a bolt, you need to select either an edge or surface for both bolt head and nut end. It is advisable to select surfaces for load bearing as they will help to produce more realistic results, by being able to spread the load more uniformly. Below is how Inventor Nastran represents bolts. Image is not to scale.

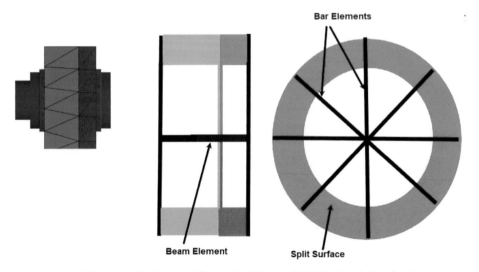

The main shank of the bolt is represented by a beam element with the same sectional properties of the bolt. Whereas the bar elements cross sectional properties are based on a half diameter of the bolt with the same material properties as the bolt.

 Adding the washers increases the effective length of the beam element by the same amount as washer heights. This will thus represent the bolt more accurately.

The preload can be defined by either specifying an axial load or torque Load. If torque is selected, you will also need to specify torque coefficient.

The formula used to calculate preload based on torque option is,

$$Preload = \frac{Torque}{Torque\ Coeficient * Bolt\ Diameter}$$

Where the torque coefficient can be found in standard engineering textbooks. Below are some typical values.

Bolt Conditions	Coefficient
Non-Plated	0.3
Zinc-Plate	0.2
Cadmium-Plate	0.16

Cap Screw

To define a cap screw, you need to specify either an edge or surface for bolt head and thread surface.

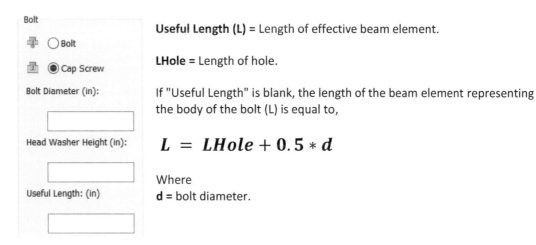

Useful Length (L) = Length of effective beam element.

LHole = Length of hole.

If "Useful Length" is blank, the length of the beam element representing the body of the bolt (L) is equal to,

$$L = LHole + 0.5 * d$$

Where

d = bolt diameter.

 Useful Length is used in situations where the geometry representing the bolt is not accurate. If specified this value will be taken as the new L value.

CHAPTER 1
The Inventor Nastran Environment

Below is how Inventor Nastran represent's cap screws. Image is not to scale.

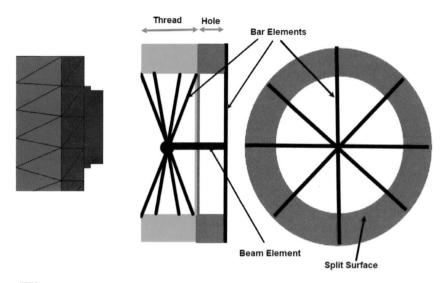

 Surface for threaded region defines the used threaded portion of the cap screw. To avoid over stiffening the model the threaded region should be split to limit the amount of surface used for threads to only the region where cap screw threads are in contact with the female threads of the body. This is demonstrated below.

Surfaces

Offset Surfaces

Within Inventor Nastran there are three methods to create surfaces from thin solids.

1. Find Thin Bodies.
2. Midsurface.
3. Offset Surfaces.

Find Thin Bodies

This tool when selected will automatically determine components to be converted to mid surfaces, Once the OK button is pressed in response to the prompt a list of the selected bodies will appear that will be converted to midsurfaces.

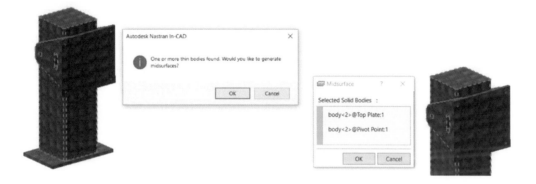

At this stage further components can be selected. Once the OK button is pressed the selected parts will be converted to midsurfaces along with the associated idealizations, with the correct thickness and material properties.

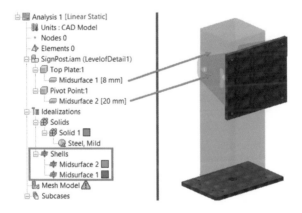

 Components with a thickness to length ratio greater than 20 will be automatically selected.

Midsurface

This command is used to select any component for which a mid-surface is required that was not automatically detected using the find thin bodies tool.

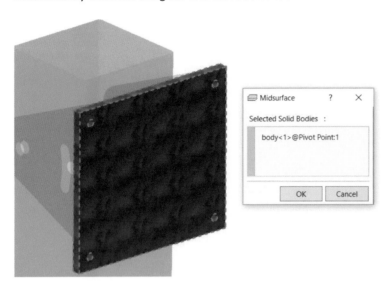

 Creating midsurfaces will create gaps between components (surfaces) so take care in interpreting results, as in reality there will be no gaps.

 If an assembly comprises of multiple parts made from the same material and are also welded together, then shrink-wrapping the assembly will simplify the analysis and surface creation.

Offset

This command unlike the midsurface gives the user control on what feature/face of the component is to be used as a surface. In this example the outside surfaces are selected and an Offset value of zero is used as we do not want to move the surfaces. In doing this one can manually specify a thickness value as shown below.

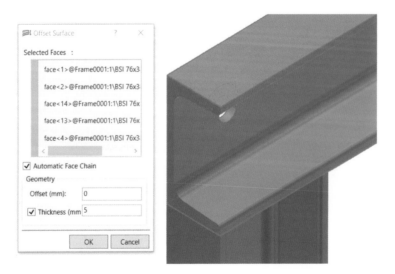

For comparison purposes below are the results of using offset and midsurface options.

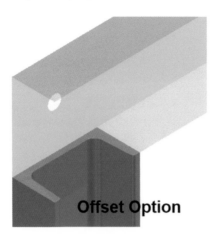

Offset Option

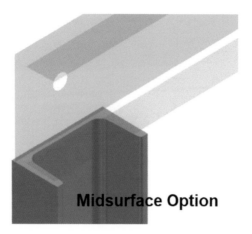

Midsurface Option

As you can clearly see the offset option produces the simplest surface representation, with the bonus of no gaps between created surfaces and adjoining components.

 Offset Surfaces can be ideally used to simplify the components for the purposes of analysis and meshing, as an alternative to suppressing features within Inventor.

 Use Offset Surfaces command if you have split faces as this command will not merge the faces.

Here I am going to illustrate the potential difference in results at connections as a result of surface creation, using different tools, for thin structures. The key feature to note is the radii of the box sections which if removed can possibly result in providing extra stiffness in the model. The box section is fixed on the far face and a load of 200N is applied on the edges of the other box section as shown below.

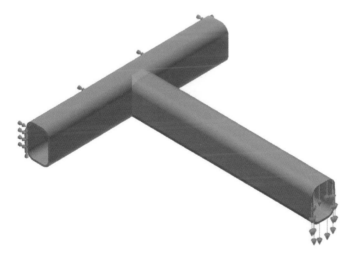

Let's have a look at the results of the model with each box section as a separate component. The first thing you will note is the gap as result of creating midsurfaces for each box section as shown below.

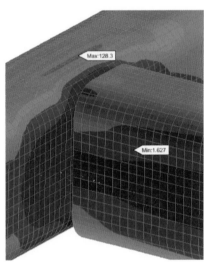

First let's look at the von-mises stress. We can clearly see there is very little stress transferred at the connection of the box sections. This also suggests that the contact elements are very stiff. You can alter the stiffness of the contact elements to get a more realistic result. In my opinion this is not straight forward and will be based on trial and error to get more realistic results at connections.

Now we are going to use offset surfaces to create a more connected surface to include the welds as well, leaving no gap between box section. Before using offset surfaces, I would suggest you create a shrink-wrap substitute of the assembly allowing us to treat the assembly as one. We can then use offset surface command as below. You can see we now have a more realistic representation of the box sections.

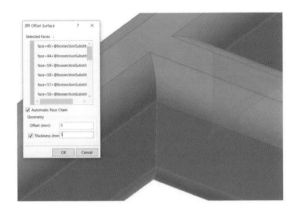
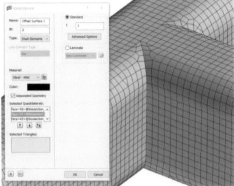

We can clearly see the results are very different. The high stresses at the connections on the left image are a more realistic representation.

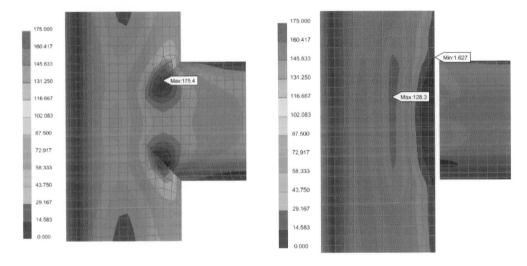

So, take care when analysing results near the gaps created using midsurfaces.

Structural Members

Structural
Members

Components created using the Inventor Frame Generator are listed within the **Structural Members** dialog as shown below. By default, they will be selected in the Beams section.

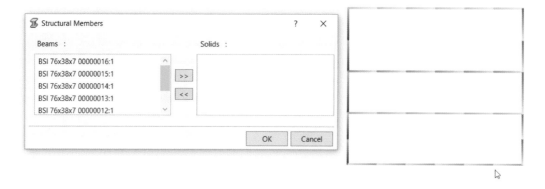

From there, you can choose whether to represent each member using beam elements or solid elements.

Beams – Lists structural members to be represented by beam elements.

Solids – Lists structural members to be represented by solid elements.

Use the double-arrow keys in between the two list boxes to move selected members from one list to the other.

Illustration below shows structures being represented by solid elements.

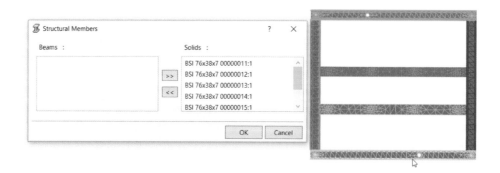

Constraints

Constraints

Inventor Nastran has the following constraints.

1. Structural.
2. Pin.
3. Frictionless
4. Response Spectrum.
5. Thermal.

Thermal and response spectrum analysis are not covered in this edition of the book.

Structural constraint

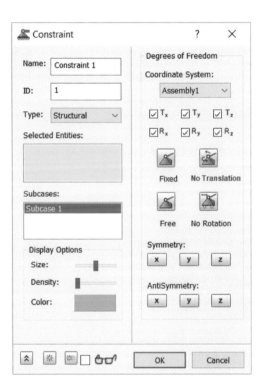

Selected Entities – A point, edge, face or surface can be selected.

Subcases – Select subcases for which the constraints are being defined.

Display Options – Allows to modify size, density and colour of the constraints.

Coordinate System – Here you can select the coordinate system of your choice including custom coordinate systems.

Fixed – When selected will fix the selected entity of the component in all 6 degrees of freedom.

No Translation – When selected will fix the selected entity of the component in 3 translational degrees of freedom.

Free – When selected components will be free to move in all directions.

No Rotation – When selected will fix the selected entity of the component in 3 rotational degrees of freedom.

Symmetry – When X, Y, Z buttons are selected Nastran will define symmetry conditions by selecting the correct degrees of freedom.

AntiSymmetry – When X, Y, Z buttons are selected Nastran will define antisymmetric conditions by selecting the correct degrees of freedom.

 Fixed and No Translation constraint yield the same result when selecting components meshed with solid elements.

Pin constraint

Selecting circular surfaces or faces with pin constraint will automatically create custom cylindrical coordinate systems. Allowing the ability to fix radial and axial directions, of the custom coordinate system, to simulate a pin connection by allowing rotation in the tangential direction.

Frictionless constraint

The location can only be defined by selecting a planar or circular face. Frictionless constraint enables a component to freely slide along a plane (or circular face) and prevent motion normal to the sliding plane (or circular face).

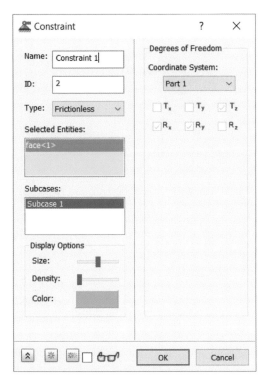

Frictionless constraints are commonly used to model symmetry boundary conditions, for example a quarter or half model.

You cannot apply frictionless constraints to edges.

When you select a face not in line with the global coordinate a new coordinate system will be generated as shown below.

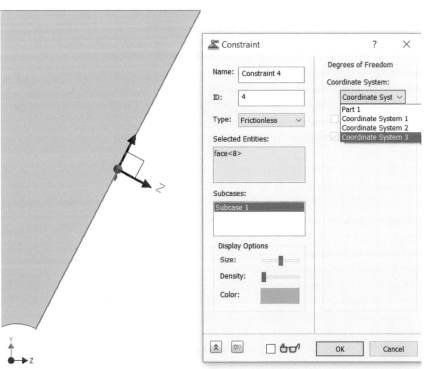

Loads

Loads

Inventor Nastran has a comprehensive list of loads covering structural and thermal loads. As this edition of the book will be focused on linear analysis we will only mention structural loads. Structural loads can be broadly classified into the following categories.

1. **General Loads**
    a. Force.
    b. Moment.
    c. Pressure.
    d. Enforced Motion.
    e. Rotational Force.
2. **Face Loads**
    a. Remote Force.
    b. Bearing Load.
3. **Edge Load**
    a. Distributed Load.
4. **Body Loads**
    a. Gravity.
5. **Hydrostatic Load**

General loads

To fully define general loads, a location, direction, and magnitude are all required. Location can be defined by selecting a face, an edge or point. Directions can be defined by either selecting a geometric entity, vector components or normal to surface option.

All general loads can be defined as variable loads, as shown below.

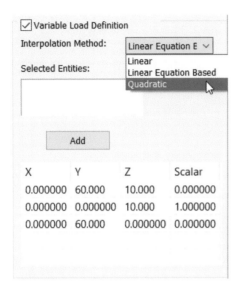

Interpolation Method – The variable load can be interpolated using either of the following methods

- Linear
- Linear Equation Based
- Quadratic

Selected Entities – To define the height or length two points need to be selected. Once defined the **Add** button can be selected. This will populate the x, y and z coordinates defining the height or length. Finally, the scalar quantities can then be specified to represent the variable load.

💡 Activate face chain for selected entities for location to quickly select adjacent faces external or internal.

📝 For linear equation based you need to specify a third point on the face or surface, where the load is being applied.

The following example illustrates the difference between the Interpolation Methods.

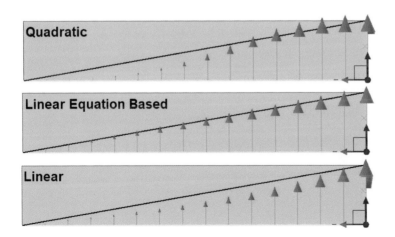

📝 Linear is not strictly linear and is more parabolic.

Enforced Motion load has an additional attribute where magnitude value can be specified by either displacement or rotation as shown below.

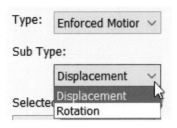

For Rotational Force load the origin of rotation also needs to be specified either using a sketch/3D Point, node or by entering X, Y, Z global coordinates. Then you specify the direction of the Rotational Vector. Load type can also be specified as velocity or acceleration.

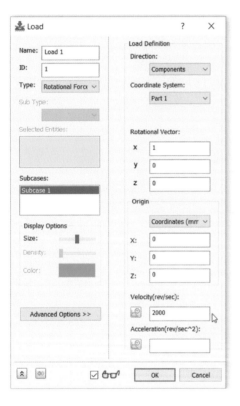

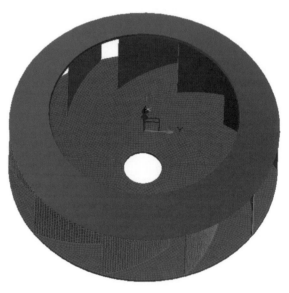

Face loads

To fully define face loads, a location, direction, and magnitude are all required. Location can only be defined by face. Direction can be defined by either selecting a geometric entity, vector components or normal to surface option.

 A bearing load can only be applied on a cylindrical face. Although the face does not have to be a complete circle.

Remote force's location can either be specified by a sketch/3D Point, node or by entering X, Y, Z global coordinates. In the example below the location is specified using coordinates.

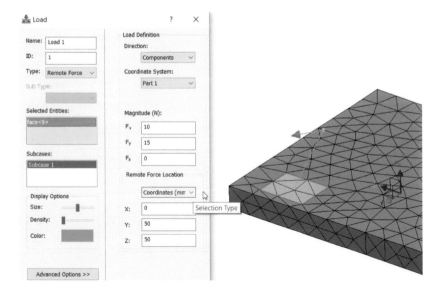

Edge load

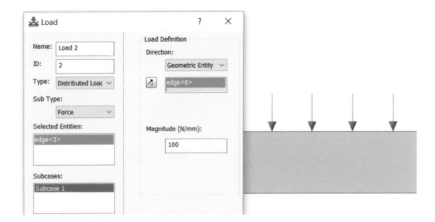

To fully define edge loads, a location, direction, and magnitude are all required. Location can only be defined by selecting an edge. Direction can be defined by either selecting a geometric entity, vector components or normal to surface option.

Body loads

To fully define body loads a direction and magnitude are only required. Direction can be defined by either selecting a geometric entity, vector components or normal to surface option. Once defined a gravity symbol will appear on the screen denoted by a g value.

Hydrostatic load

Hydrostatic pressure varies linearly from the surface level of the fluid in the direction of increasing depth of the fluid.

Hydrostatic pressure = (fluid density) x (depth below the fluid surface).

Hydrostatic Load is used in scenarios when we want to simulate pressure being exerted on structures by fluid, like water. To fully define hydrostatic load, we need to define location of load, fluid direction, position of fluid surface and density. In pressurized containers/tanks you will need to also define pressure.

You can apply hydrostatic pressure to faces of shells and solids. The pressure is normal to the face of the elements.

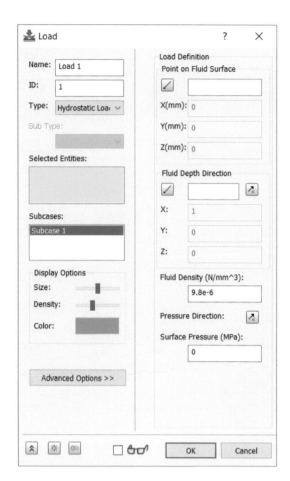

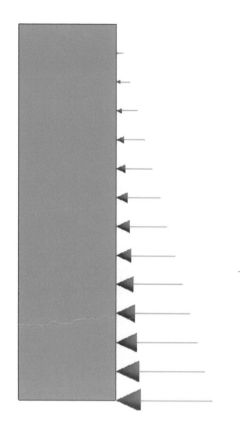

Point on Fluid Surface – Can be defined, either by selecting an entity in the model, or by using the X, Y, and Z fields. Only elements below this point receive a hydrostatic pressure.

Fluid Depth Direction – Can be defined, either by selecting an entity in the model, or by using the X, Y, and Z fields.

Fluid Density – Specify the weight density of the fluid that causes the pressure.

Surface Pressure – Defines the pressure on top of the fluid, such as a pressurized vessel partially filled with liquid. The pressure above the fluid surface is equal to the surface pressure. The pressure below the fluid surface is equal to the surface pressure plus the hydrostatic pressure.

Contacts tab

 Auto

 Manual

Solver

There are seven types of contacts available within Inventor Nastran.

Types of contacts

1. **Bonded** – Bonds contact faces to each other, for example, in fabricated structures.

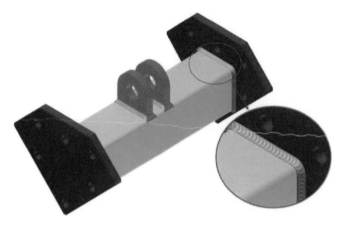

2. **Separation** – Allows adjacent contact faces to separate and slide under deformation; for example, hole pin connection.

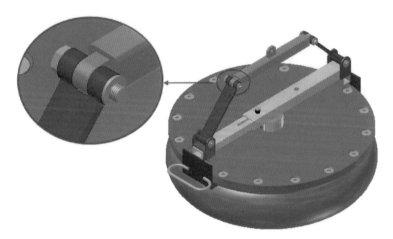

3. **Sliding/No Separation** – Maintains contact between adjacent faces and allows sliding when under deformation.

4. **Separation / No Sliding** – Separates contact faces partially or fully without sliding.

5. **Shrink Fit / Sliding** – Similar to Separation contact with the addition of allowing for initial overlaps between components creating prestress conditions.

6. **Shrink Fit / No Sliding** – Is like a Separation / No Sliding contact but with initial interference between the contacting parts. Use this type when the intensity of fit and friction are great enough to prevent relative motion (sliding) between the contacting parts.

> Shrink Fit contacts should have at least two subcases defined, and the first subcase should have no defined loads. Loads can be defined for other subcases. This setup allows Nastran to solve for interference until an equilibrium is achieved with minimal contact penetration for the initial subcase. Then the external load is applied on the prestressed subcase 1.

7. **Offset Bonded** – To simulate welded connections with significant separation between contacting surfaces as shown below.

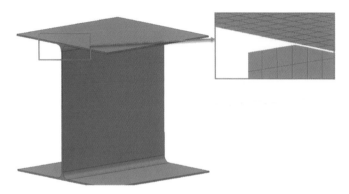

> Always use offset bonded contacts for surfaces created using midsurfaces.

The process of creating contacts

There are three methods to create contacts.

1. Automatically.
2. Manually.
3. Solver based contacts.

Automatic Contacts

This method creates contact pairs between adjacent faces/surfaces/edges based on the tolerance value set within the analysis settings.

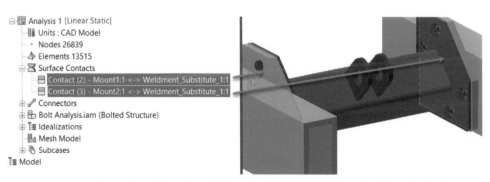

Manual Contacts

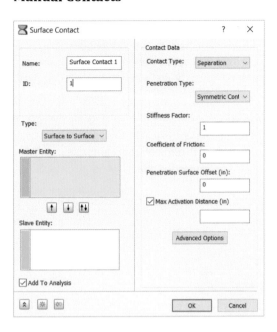

Type – Manual contacts can be created between two surfaces and between surfaces and edges.

Master Entity – Only surfaces or faces can be selected for master.

Slave Entity – Both Surfaces and edges can be selected for slave.

Penetration Type – Symmetric Contact is the default option and is more accurate than the Unsymmetric Contact. As it detects for penetration between both slave and master and vice versa.

Stiffness Factor – Controls the stiffness scaling of the contact and is automatically determined based on the adjacent stiffness. A higher value will produce less penetration and, in some case, if the value is to high then this can lead to convergence issues.

Coefficient of Friction – Here you can specify a static friction value to simulate reality between components more accurately.

Penetration Surface Offset – This defines a numerical offset value for instances such as plate to plate or solid to plate contact

Max Activation Distance – Here you specify a value which Inventor Nastran uses to maintain contact.
This helps limit the number of contact elements and therefore decreases solution time, prevents unnecessary and possibly conflicting contact elements. Leaving it blank will create more contacts leading to longer solve times.

 You always need to specify a value when using offset bonded contacts.

Specify a value which covers the biggest gap between mid-surfaces, automatically generated.

Solver based contacts

Solver based contact is an automatic based process and contacts are created/activated during the solve time.

Specify Contact Regions – Here you can specify the contact pairs to help limit the number of contacts automatically created.

In addition to the manual contact properties the solver contact gives you two more properties to consider.

Max Allowable Penetration – This is used in the adjustment of penalty values normal to the contact plane. A positive value activates the penalty value adjustment.

Frictional Stiffness for Stick – (This info is obtained from Inventor Nastran online help) The value of frictional stiffness should be chosen carefully. A method of choosing a value is to divide the expected frictional strength (MU X Expected normal force) by reasonable value of the relative displacement before slip occurs. A large stiffness value may cause poor convergence, while too small a value may result in reduced accuracy. An alternative method is to specify the value of relative displacement using SMAX.

 Apart from contact type you only ever need to specify coefficient of friction and max activation distance when required.

Mesh

1. Mesh Settings.
2. Table.
3. Generate Mesh.
4. Mesh control.
5. Convergence Settings

Mesh Settings

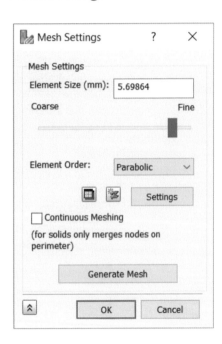

Mesh Settings will apply to all areas of the component and all components of an assembly. This is known as Global Meshing.

Element Size (mm) – Here the maximum size of the element can be specified for a part or an assembly. The slider can also be used to select an element size.

Element Order – Within Inventor Nastran a parabolic or linear element can be specified. Mathematically a parabolic element is more accurate than a linear element.

The following illustrations show that one parabolic (quadratic) element around a 90^0 circular arc is like having two linear elements. The parabolic (quadratic) element tries to match the 90^0 arc more closely and can also improve the accuracy of results.

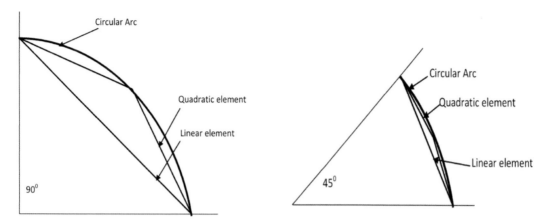

Also, it is worth noting that the parabolic element almost matches the true profile of a 45^0 curved object (< 1% geometrical error). Therefore, it is advisable to have at least two quadratic elements around a 90^0 arc, whereas for linear elements there should be at least three elements, preferably four, around a 90^0 circular object.

Continuous Meshing – When selected merges nodes of elements at the intersection of surfaces.

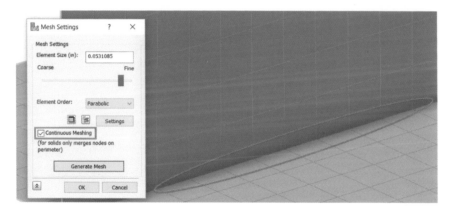

Continuous meshing helps to avoid the need for using contacts.

Settings – Enables you to apply further advanced control.

Tolerance – In the event of mesh failures altering this value can help to generate a successful mesh.

Refinement Ratio – Adjusting to a smaller value can help to generate more elements around small features. It also helps to create more uniformity in the mesh. Below you can see by altering the refinement ratio to 0.1 we can capture small feature representations more accurately with the mesh.

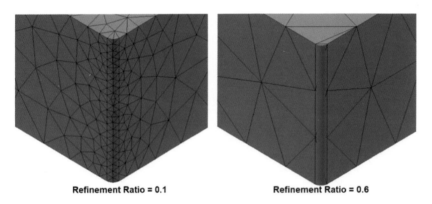

Refinement Ratio = 0.1   Refinement Ratio = 0.6

An alternative approach to capturing small features is to use mesh control.

Min Angle Tolerance – Controls how much the minimum angles of mesh elements are allowed to vary.

Max Angle Tolerance – Controls how much the maximum angles of mesh element are allowed to vary. A higher value will produce a more uniform mesh distribution.

Max Element Growth Rate – Controls the maximum length of the adjacent element edges for transitioning between coarse and fine regions. A smaller value than the default, will produce a more uniform mesh as illustrated below.

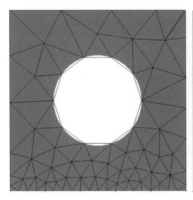 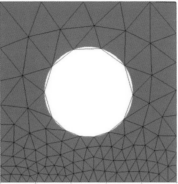

Element Growth Rate = 1.5   **Element Growth Rate = 1.2**

 Use 1.05 as the lowest value.

Suppress Short Features – Suppresses or covers up small features.

Min Feature Angle – Controls the angle of mesh elements around different features

Project Midside Nodes – When selected will project midside nodes of parabolic elements onto curved geometry as shown below.

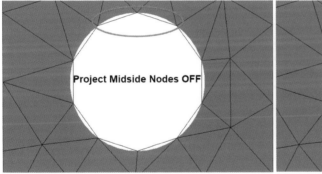 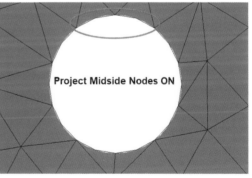

Quality Midside Adjustment – Controls midside adjustment and adjusts mesh if necessary.

Upper Jacobian Ratio Bound: Ratio that governs quality midside adjustment.

 Refinement ratio, max element growth rate and project midside nodes settings are only required in most cases to help achieve convergence in mesh results.

Table

Part Name – Is the name of component.

Visibility – Allows you to switch the mesh visibility on or off.

Color – Is the colour of the mesh as defined by the idealization.

Size (mm) – Here you can specify the size of the element for each part. This will over-ride the mesh size in the settings dialogue box once you press generate mesh.

Tolerance (mm) – You can specify individual tolerance values.

Element Order – Here you have ability to specify linear or parabolic element for each part.

Settings – Access and set advance settings related to the part only.

Nodes – Displays the number of nodes generated.

Elements – Displays the number of elements generated.

☑ – The checkbox column selects all or individual parts for editing. You can toggle the state of the checkboxes for individual parts or click the checkbox in the header to toggle the select or deselect all parts in a single click. Once checked you can either select Generate Mesh or Delete button. If you have multiple parts selected, then you will not be able to select the setting button to access advanced settings. However, you will be able to modify all other properties in the table in a single operation.

Zoom (🔍) – Select this icon to zoom to part.

Generate Mesh

Select this button to generate or update mesh. You must regenerate the mesh whenever a change is made in the model. A progress bar visually indicates the progress of the meshing operation.

Local Mesh Control

Local mesh control allows you to control mesh sizes by selecting points, edges, faces and parts in the case of an assembly. This is further illustrated below.

Manual Mesh Convergence

It is important to note that stress results can significantly change due to changes in mesh size. So, it's important that you carry out analyses using different mesh sizes. I would recommend you take the following approach.

1. Run analysis with default mesh size.
2. Rerun analysis with half the default mesh size.
3. Rerun analysis by further halving the mesh size in step 2.
4. Rerun analysis if difference in value is close to 10% between the analysis results of step 2 and 3.

 Use local mesh control and max element growth rate settings for step 4.

If the difference between the first and last analysis is within 10%, you can assume that your results have converged. It's important that at least the last 2 analysis results are within 10%.

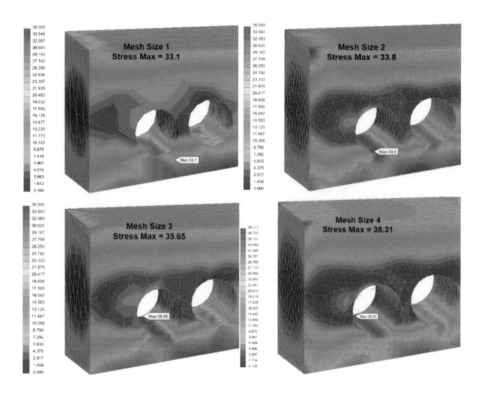

Automatic Mesh Convergence

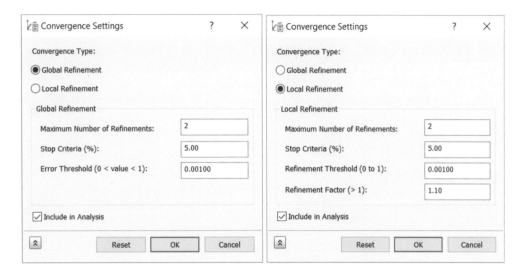

Global Refinement

This type of refinement creates a finer uniform mesh at each progressive iteration all over the model as shown below.

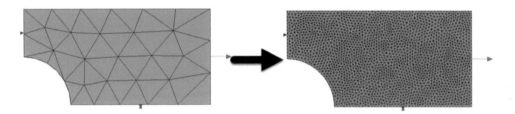

Maximum Number of Refinements

Specifies the maximum number of h refinement cycles for convergence. Default value is 5.

 Use a maximum value of 2 for global mesh refinement.

Stop Criteria (%)

Sets a minimum percentage value for the difference between subsequent refinement results.

 Von Mises stress results are used for Stop Criteria.

Error Threshold (0 < value < 1)

Is a value between 0 and 1 that stops the refinement if the calculated strain energy error is less than the specified threshold value? The strain energy calculated is based on the following equation and compared with the error threshold value.

$$Error = sqrt(seerr/setot)$$
$$seer = Strain\ energy\ error$$
$$setot = Total\ strain\ energy + strain\ energy$$

 For setting the error threshold value, it is recommended to run the first analysis with a threshold value of 0.01.

Local Refinement

Here the mesh around the high stress areas will only be refined based on the following settings.

Maximum Number of Refinements

Specifies the maximum number of h refinement cycles for convergence. Default value is 5.

Stop Criteria (%)

Sets a minimum percentage value for the difference between subsequent refinement results.

 Von Mises stress results are used for Stop Criteria

Refinement Threshold (0 to 1)

This value will determine how many elements within the model will be used by the local mesh refinement? A value of 0 would include all elements (similar to global mesh control), while a setting of 1 would include no elements.

The default of 0.95 will refine the top 5% of the elements.

Refinement Factor (> 1)

This works as the same way as the Max Element Growth Rate within the Advance Mesh Settings.

Include in Analysis needs to be checked to activate Automatic Mesh Convergence.

Run

Run

Once the setup has completed the next step is the click on the Run button. Once complete results will become available.

Results

Load Results

By default, the results are not uploaded automatically. By selecting this button, you can load results by selecting the .FNO results file. In cases where multiple analyses exist it may not be so obvious to match the correct results files with the active analysis. An alternative method to load results is to right click on results and then select Load Results.

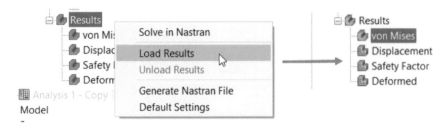

Contour

This button is selected by default and displays solid von Mises stress results by default, which can be easily modified to display another result using the results navigation bar.

CONTOUR: SOLID VON MISES STRESS (MPa)
OUTPUT SET: SUBCASE 1

Deformed

This button is selected by default and displays results using a deformation scale of 10%.

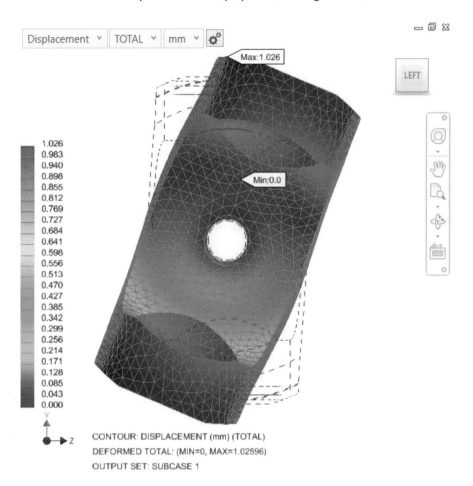

The red dashed line represents undeformed shape.

Return

This button when selected will go back to the Nastran pre-processing environment.

Stress Linearization

Stress Linearization is used to comply with design codes and requirements of the pressure vessel industry.

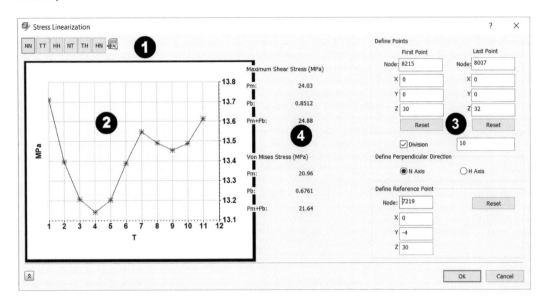

The Stress Linearization utility dialog can be broken down into the following sections.

1. Local Stress Tensors.
2. Stress Linearization Graph.
3. Linearization Controls.
4. Stress Linearization Results.

Local Stress Tensors

These selections allow you to choose which result to plot in the graph.

Where:

1. The first letter of the tensor refers to the vector normal to the face of the element
2. The second letter is the direction of the stress.

For example, NN is the normal stress in the local N direction and TH is the shear stress along the HN plane in the H direction.

CHAPTER 1
The Inventor Nastran Environment

Stress Linearization Graph

The graph displays the local stress tensor results along the currently defined Stress Classification Line (SCL).

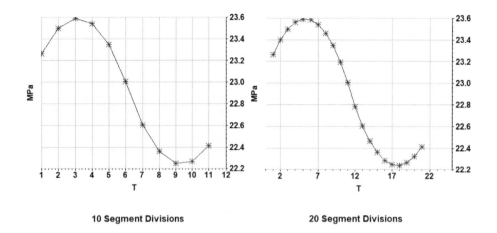

| 10 Segment Divisions | 20 Segment Divisions |

The SCL is divided into 10 segments by default which you can override. The results are calculated from the stress tensor values and output at each point.

Linearization Controls:

The linearization controls allow you to specify the first and last point to define the SCL. Including the ability to define the orientation of the local stress tensor graph. The figure below shows the local axis configuration if the N Axis is defined, and the T axis direction is not inverted

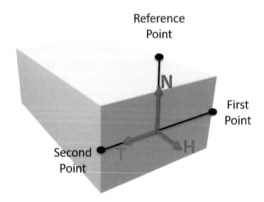

All the points can be defined by any of the following methods

- Specifying the node number, if known, into Node field.

- Graphically selected the node from the model.

- Specifying the coordinates of any point on the model into the X, Y, and Z fields.

Stress Linearization Results

Results are displayed for both the Maximum Shear Stress and the Von Mises Stress. Refer to the following link for more information from the online help.

http://help.autodesk.com/view/NINCAD/2019/ENU/?guid=GUID-F7AE330B-20F8-42F5-A1D4-F2E95AEA156C

Subcase Results

This button allows you to quickly see the results from each subcase by selecting the next and previous buttons, rather than selecting from the browser.

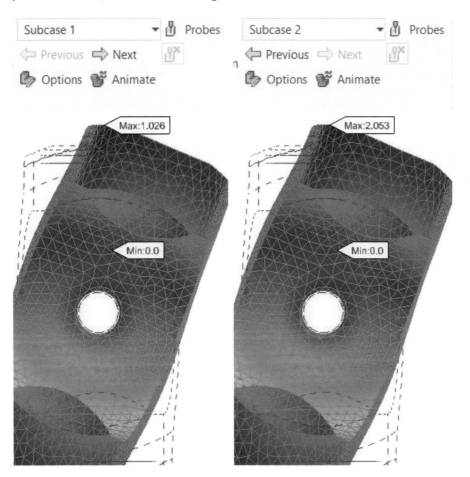

Animate

When selected will animate the currently displayed results using the default settings. To stop animation, just deselect the animate button.

CHAPTER 1
The Inventor Nastran Environment

Options

This can be accessed by clicking on the options button in the results panel or by right clicking any of the default result plots in the browser.

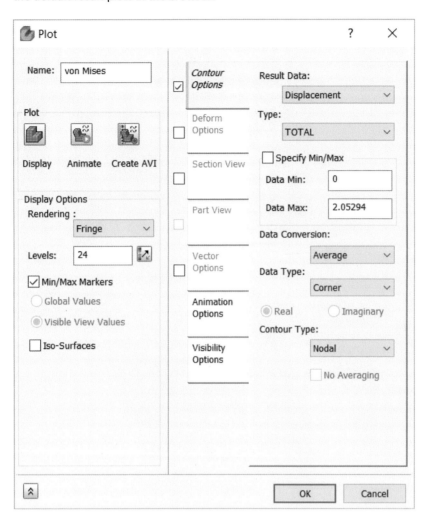

Display – Select to display results.

Animate – Select to animate results.

Create AVI – Select to create a video of the results.

Rendering – Nastran currently allows you to display results using any of the following options.

- Line.
- Fringe.
- Continuous.
- Gouraud.

Line – Contour lines are plotted on the surface of the model according to the number of levels on the contour plot legend as shown below.

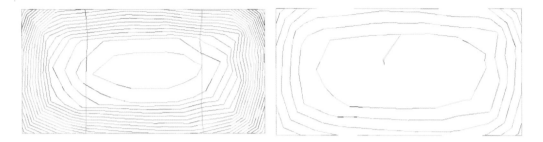

Fringe – Displays results on surface of the model similarly to the number of levels of the legend plot.

Continuous – Displays smooth results on surface of the model by blending the colours naturally from one node to the next node. The number of levels does not have any impact on continuous results.

Gouraud – Also displays smooth results similarly to continuous. The difference between the two methods is subtle and can be affected by light source acting on the model. Again, the number of levels does not affect the results.

CHAPTER 1
The Inventor Nastran Environment

Levels – Here you set the number of levels of the contour plot legend. The maximum number allowed is 252 levels.

 This Flip Color button will invert the legend colours.

Min/Max Markers – will display maximum and minimum values on the model. When Section or Part View mode is active, the following two additional options are also available.

Global Values – will display maximum and minimum values even if the areas of these results are not currently displayed.

Visible View Values – will display maximum and minimum values considering only the currently visible portion of the model. When this option is chosen, the actual minimum and maximum result for the full model may differ from the values shown.

Iso-Surfaces – This option, when checked, displays surfaces controlled by the levels of contour plot legend.

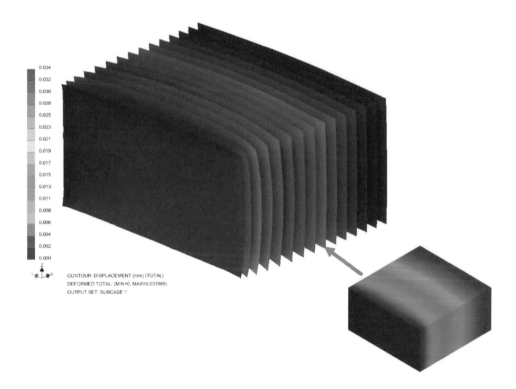

Contour Options

Has the following main sections.

1. Result Data.
2. Type.
3. Specify Min/Max.
4. Data Conversion.
5. Data Type.
6. Contour Type.

Result Data – This displays the following list of results

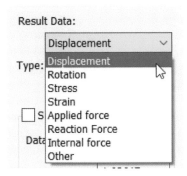

Below is a brief explanation of some of the solid element results available for linear stress analysis.

RESULT TYPE	EXPLANATION
SOLID X, Y, Z - NORMAL STRESS	Directional stress based on the part coordinate system.
SOLID XY, YZ, ZX - SHEAR STRESS	Planar shear stresses based on the part coordinate system.
SOLID PRINCIPAL – A STRESS	Maximum principal stress.
SOLID PRINCIPAL – C STRESS	Minimum principal stress.
SOLID PRINCIPAL – B STRESS	Median principal stress.
SOLID VON MISES STRESS	Takes all stresses into consideration, including bending, shear and axial. Most commonly used stress result.
SOLID MAX SHEAR STRESS	Maximum shear stress.
SOLID MAX PRINICIPAL STRESS	Most tensile stress.
SOLID MIN PRINCIPAL STRESS	Most compressive stress.

CHAPTER 1

The Inventor Nastran Environment

Further explanation of all result types can be accessed from the Nastran help file and using the link below.

http://help.autodesk.com/view/NSTRN/2019/ENU/?guid=GUID-87399188-B8F0-4233-9FE2-1D670D440725

Type – The contents of this list is dependent on the results data and the analysis type. Below is the list based on displacement results data.

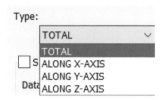

Specify Min/Max – When selected allows you to specify the minimum and maximum values of contour plot legend. Contour plot colours will then adjust according to the new range.

All contour areas above the specified maximum value will be red, and those below the minimum value will be blue if the rendering is set to continuous or gouraud. If rendering is set to line or fringe the results above the maximum value will be greyed out as shown below.

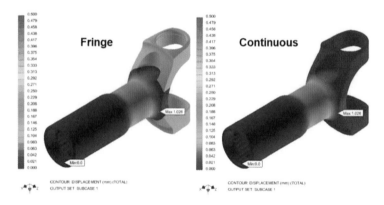

💡 Use specify min/max when you have stress singularities present in the model to isolate them from the area of interest.

Data Conversion – In the case of multiple results at nodal locations Data Conversions lets you choose how to combine the results to be used in results plots.

Average – Takes average value of all nodal values at a location.

Maximum – Takes maximum value of all nodal values at a location.

Minimum – Takes minimum value of all nodal values at a location.

💡 If there is a large difference between the three values, then you need to further refine mesh.

Data Type – Allows you to select whether you would like to use nodal or elemental results.

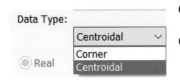

Corner – Results based on the corner nodal values of the element.

Centroidal – Results based on the nodal average of the elements.

Contour Type – This section allows you to select whether you want the results to be displayed on the nodes or elements.

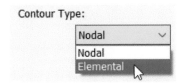

Nodal – This averages all the nodes at a location resulting in a smooth mesh. Nodal Contour results cannot account for any discontinuities in material or geometry. Can also loose accuracy at material boundaries.

Elemental – Results are not as smooth as Nodal. Elemental results are useful for assemblies with multiple materials or shell elements that intersect at large angles. Also useful for variable shell idealizations and viewing top and bottom results for shell elements.

No Averaging – is highlighted when Elemental is selected for Contour type. The results are not averaged with adjacent elements resulting in discontinuous contour plot. With this option you are looking at raw data as no averaging of data takes place.

Let's take the following four elements and their nodal/centroidal values to best explain the above settings and their impact on the stress results value.

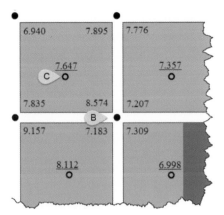

💡 Displacement results are same at the nodes and thus are not affected by changing the Data Conversion, Data Type and Contour Type settings.

Data Conversion	Data Type	Contour Type	No Averaging	Description	Displayed	Results
Average	Corner	Nodal	N/A	Average of all values at a node location	@ Node	@ B (8.574+7.207+7.183+7.309)/4 = 7.568
Average	Corner	Elemental	Unselected	Same as above	@ Node	Same as above
Average	Corner	Elemental	Selected	All nodes on element are averaged	@ Element	@ C (6.940+7.895+8.574+7.835)/4 = 7.811
Average	Centroidal	Nodal	N/A	Average value from all elements attached at a node	@ Node	@ B (7.647+7.357+6.998+8.112)/4 = 7.529
Average	Centroidal	Elemental	Unselected	Same as above	@ Node	Same as above
Average	Centroidal	Elemental	Selected	Element centroidal results	@ Element	7.647 @ C
Maximum	Corner	Nodal	N/A	Maximum of all values at a node location	@ Node	8.574 @ B as being the maximum value
Maximum	Corner	Elemental	Unselected	Same as above	@ Node	Same as above
Maximum	Corner	Elemental	Selected	Nodal max of element	@ Element	8.574 @ C
Maximum	Centroidal	Nodal	N/A	Maximum value from all elements attached at a node	@ Node	8.112 @ B as being the maximum value

Data Conversion	Data Type	Contour Type	No Averaging	Description	Result Type	Result
Maximum	Centroidal	Elemental	Unselected	Same as above	@ Node	Same as above
Maximum	Centroidal	Elemental	Selected	Element centroidal results	@ Element	7.647 @ C
Minimum	Corner	Nodal	N/A	Minimum of all values at a node location	@ Node	7.183 @ B as being the minimum value
Minimum	Corner	Elemental	Unselected	Same as above	@ Node	Same as above
Minimum	Corner	Elemental	Selected	Nodal min of element	@ Element	6.940 @ C
Minimum	Centroidal	Nodal	N/A	Minimum value from all elements attached at a node	@ Node	6.998 @ B as being the minimum value
Minimum	Centroidal	Elemental	Unselected	Same as above	@ Node	Same as before
Minimum	Centroidal	Elemental	Selected	Element centroidal results	@ Element	7.647 @ C

Deform Options

This tab has the following options.

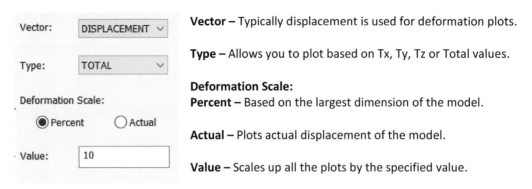

Vector – Typically displacement is used for deformation plots.

Type – Allows you to plot based on Tx, Ty, Tz or Total values.

Deformation Scale:
Percent – Based on the largest dimension of the model.

Actual – Plots actual displacement of the model.

Value – Scales up all the plots by the specified value.

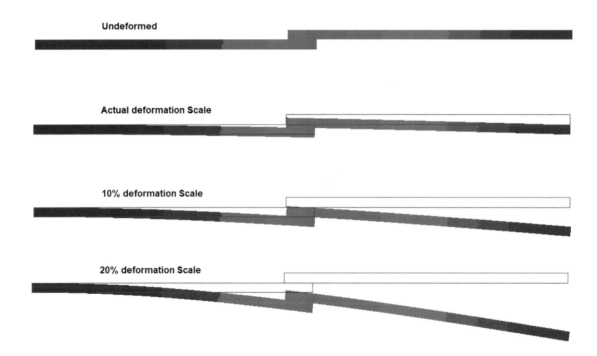

Section View

This allows you to create section views of the model.

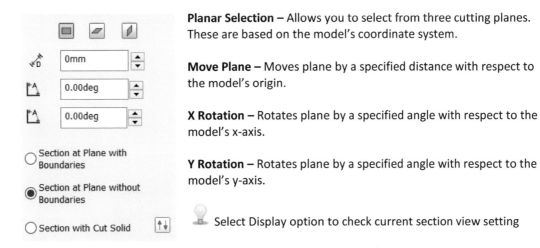

Planar Selection – Allows you to select from three cutting planes. These are based on the model's coordinate system.

Move Plane – Moves plane by a specified distance with respect to the model's origin.

X Rotation – Rotates plane by a specified angle with respect to the model's x-axis.

Y Rotation – Rotates plane by a specified angle with respect to the model's y-axis.

Select Display option to check current section view setting

Section at Plane with Boundaries – Produces a 2D plane shown as intersecting with the outline of the 3D model.

Section at Plane without Boundaries – Produce a 2D plane as shown below.

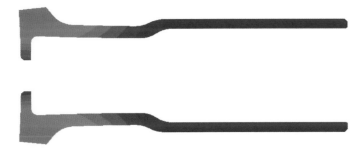

Section with Cut Solid – Displays results as shown below.

 Select to reverse the section direction if needed.

Part View
Is only available when working with assemblies and has the following options.

Select Parts – Select individual parts of the assembly that you only want displayed.

 This enables you to hide non-critical parts of an assembly when viewing results.

Vector Options

Here you can plot vectors for different results including the ability the change the size of the vectors.

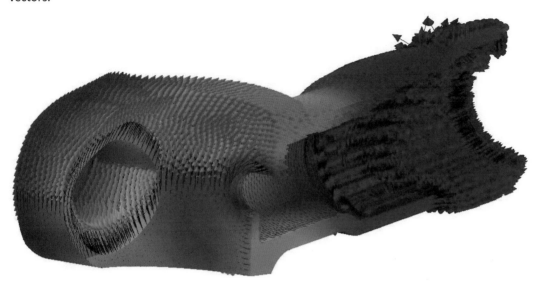

Animation Options

Here you set the options used for animations.

Number of Frames:

10

Delay (msec):

200

Mode: Full

☐ Spline Interpolation

Number of Frames – Specify the number of frames required.

Delay (msec) – Specify time between frames.

Mode

Half – The animation is set between zero and full load and then starts again from zero load.

Full – The animation is set between zero and full load and then reverses from full to zero load.

Oscillate – This option is applicable only for single-set animations. The first half of the animation is the same as a Full animation. Then, one more full animation cycle is added, except that the deformation results are inverted (positive displacements become negative displacements, and vice versa).

Spline Interpolation – For multi-set animations, interpolates intermediate outputs, increasing the number of frames to match the number specified.

Visibility Options

These options allow you to hide or show objects using the flip button. Blue button is show and black button is hide.

Element Edges:

Loads:

Constraints:

Connectors:

Concentrated Masses:

Coordinate Systems:

Free Edges:

Show All   Hide All

Probe

Using probe, you can add additional probes to the maximum and minimum value. Probe helps to pinpoint the key areas of interest in the model, especially when the model has maximum results distorted, due to stress singularities.

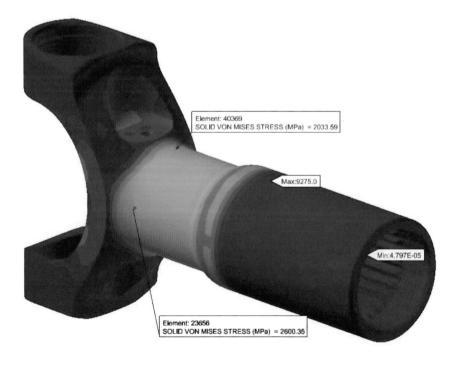

Element: 40369
SOLID VON MISES STRESS (MPa) = 2033.59

Max:9275.0

Min:4.797E-05

Element: 23656
SOLID VON MISES STRESS (MPa) = 2600.35

Convergence Plot

After running an analysis that includes mesh convergence, this plot is included in the Results panel.

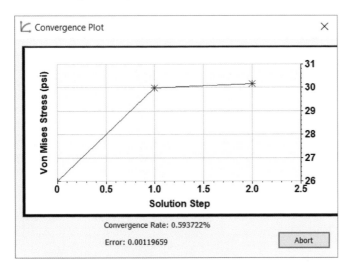

The dynamic plot shows the following details:

- The number of steps required for the solution to converge as shown above.

- The von Mises stress values associated with each refinement step.

- The convergence rate in the form of an XY plot and a percentage value.

- The strain energy error, which is useful for determining the error threshold for global mesh refinement

Object Visibility

Object Visibility

Here you have the option to hide or show objects. To hide object simply untick them from the list.

When Results are not displayed

When Results are displayed

All FEA Entities – This allows you to select multiple objects in a single click. The following items are part of FEA Entities option.

- Concentrated Masses.
- Connectors.
- Constraints.
- Coordinate Systems.
- Loads.
- Material Orientations.
- Mesh.
- Mesh Controls.

Free Edges – This option highlights the free edges of shell elements by overlaying them with a heavy white line. Free edges are those that are not mated with an adjacent shell element edge. This option is useful for finding improperly connected shell elements where faces intersect each other.

Mesh – This option controls visibility of the finite element mesh. When displaying results contours, this command is equivalent to the Element Edges option within the Visibility Options tab of the Plot and Multiset Animation Settings dialogs.

Min/Max Markers – This option controls visibility of the minimum and maximum probes.

Probes – This option controls the visibility of any user added probes.

Undeformed Edges – This controls the visibility of the undeformed shape represented by red dashed lines.

Nastran Support

Help

Here you can access the comprehensive on-line help for Nastran In-CAD.

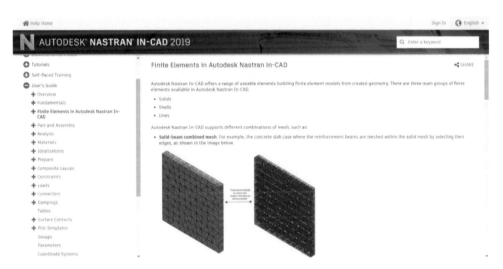

Clicking on the question mark, available in all dialogue boxes as shown below, is the quickest way to find relevant information.

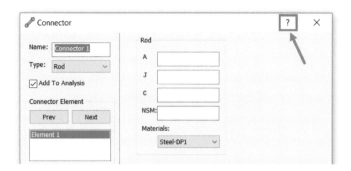

You can also access the Nastran help file for more guidance on specific Nastran related queries using the following link.

http://help.autodesk.com/view/NSTRN/2019/ENU/

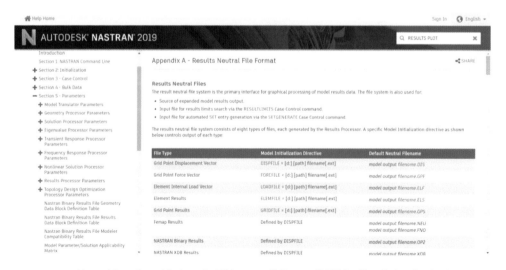

Tutorials

Here you can access additional exercises to this book.

⊖ Tutorials

   About Tutorials

   ➕ Basic Analysis Tutorials

   ➕ Advanced Analysis Tutorials

⊖ Self-Paced Training

   Self-Paced Training

   Section 1: Introducing Autodesk Nastran In-CAD

   ➕ Section 2: The Basics of Finite Element Analysis (FEA)

   ➕ Section 14: Nonlinear Static Analysis

   ➕ Section 20: Dynamic Analysis

On line exercises include basic and advanced topics including non-linear, thermal, ilogic and more.

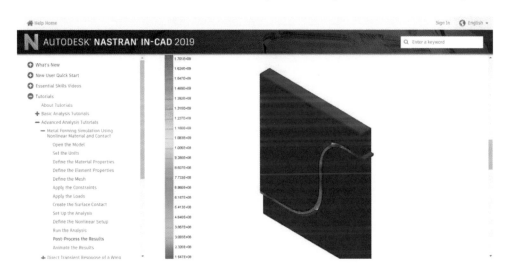

About

This provides information about your Inventor Nastran license.

Read Me

Provides further information about the current version of Inventor Nastran, including what's new and current issues.

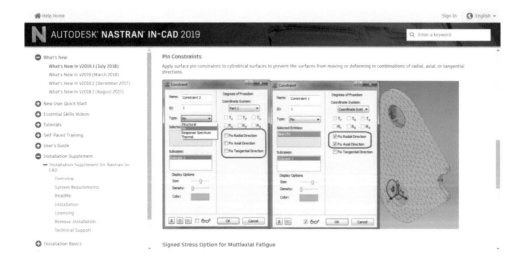

Forum

A dedicated forum where you can post Inventor Nastran related questions and get answers to, from fellow peers and Autodesk employees.

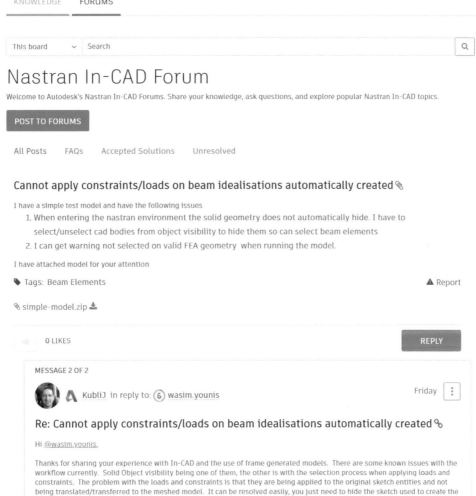

AUTODESK
NASTRAN IN-CAD

KNOWLEDGE   FORUMS

| This board ∨ | Search | 🔍 |

Nastran In-CAD Forum

Welcome to Autodesk's Nastran In-CAD Forums. Share your knowledge, ask questions, and explore popular Nastran In-CAD topics.

POST TO FORUMS

All Posts   FAQs   Accepted Solutions   Unresolved

Cannot apply constraints/loads on beam idealisations automatically created 🔗

I have a simple test model and have the following issues

1. When entering the nastran environment the solid geometry does not automatically hide. I have to select/unselect cad bodies from object visibility to hide them so can select beam elements
2. I can get warning not selected on valid FEA geometry when running the model.

I have attached model for your attention

🏷 Tags: Beam Elements   ⚠ Report

🔗 simple-model.zip ⬇

| 👍 | 0 LIKES | | **REPLY** |

MESSAGE 2 OF 2

KubliJ in reply to: ⑥ wasim.younis   Friday ⋮

Re: Cannot apply constraints/loads on beam idealisations automatically created 🔗

Hi @wasim.younis,

Thanks for sharing your experience with In-CAD and the use of frame generated models. There are some known issues with the workflow currently. Solid Object visibility being one of them, the other is with the selection process when applying loads and constraints. The problem with the loads and constraints is that they are being applied to the original sketch entities and not being translated/transferred to the meshed model. It can be resolved easily, you just need to hide the sketch used to create the frame. A more detailed explanation can be found here.

DP1 – Part Analysis – Lever Arm

(Design problem courtesy of Magnet Schultz Limited)

Key features and workflows introduced in this design problem

	Key Features/Workflows
1	Pin Constraint
2	Bearing Load
3	Basic Mesh Settings
4	Global and Local Face Mesh Control
5	Results Convergence – Manual Mesh Sensitivity Study
6	Safety Factor Result Plots
7	Redesign

Introduction

Magnet Schultz Ltd are the leading solenoid specialists in UK since 1967 and have high profile customers in a variety of industries including defence and automotive security. Typical products designed by Magnet Schultz include the T61 Right-angle Solenoid Shot bolts as shown below.

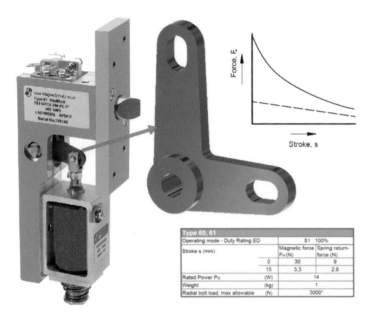

Type 60, 61				
Operating mode - Duty Rating ED			S1 100%	
Stroke s (mm)			Magnetic force F_M (N)	Spring return-force (N)
		0	30	9
		15	3.3	2.8
Rated Power P_{20}	(W)		14	
Weight	(kg)		1	
Radial bolt load, max allowable	(N)		3000*	

In this design problem we are going to analyse the lever using the following design information and goal.

Design Information

Material of Lever - **Steel**
Density - **7850kg/m³**
Youngs Modulus - **200GPa**
Poisson's Ratio - **0.29**
Yield Limit - **200MPa**
Load - **30N**
Minimum Safety Factor - **5**

Design Goal
Is to optimise the design of the lever by removing as much material as possible.

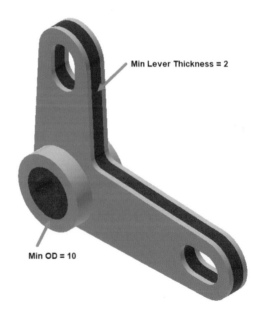

Workflow of Design Problem 1

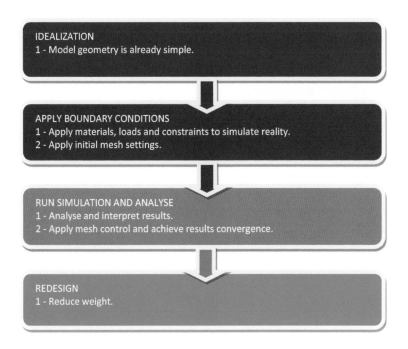

Idealization

The part file is already simple and therefore does not need to go through any further idealization.

1. Open *Lever.ipt*

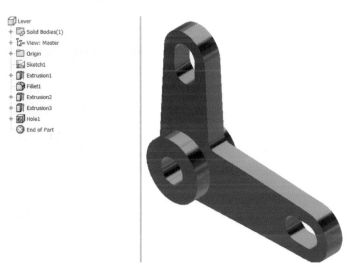

2. Apply a new material to the lever with the following properties.

 Select Mild Steel and then modify the individual properties as below within Inventor Nastran.

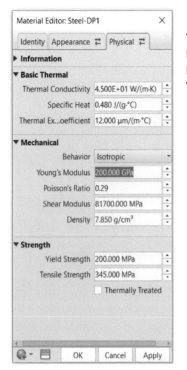

Youngs Modulus - **200GPa**
Poisson's Ratio - **0.29**
Density - **7850kg/m³**
Yield Limit – **200MPa**

Shear Modulus value is not required by Inventor Nastran, as it calculates the value using material data. In Inventor we cannot leave the field blank. Inventor Nastran will automatically remove this value.

3. Rename material **Steel-DP1**.

Boundary conditions

4. Select **Environments** tab > Select **Autodesk Inventor Nastran**.

5. Double Click **Steel-DP1** under Materials node in the Model tree.

You can see the G field is blanked out. Here you can amend or add further values as required. Any additional data defined will be saved only within the part file.

💡 You can save new materials within Nastran In-CAD that can then be accessed from other files.

6. Click **OK** > Select **Pin Constraints** > Specify **Centre–Pivot** for Name > Select highlighted cylindrical face to apply constraint > Select both **Fix Radial Direction** and **Fix Axial Direction** > Select **Preview** so you can adjust display options as desired.

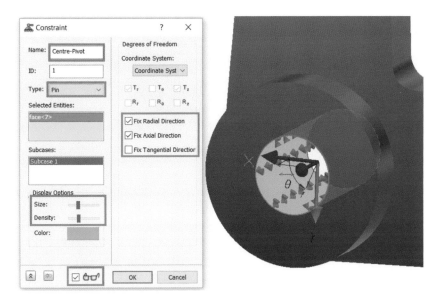

📝 Applying a pin constraint will automatically create a customised cylindrical coordinate system with reference to the selected cylindrical face.

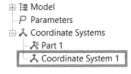

7. Select **Duplicate**.

Centre–Pivot constraint has been created and now you can define a new constraint using same settings.

8. Right click within the Selected Entities box > Select **Clear All** to remove current selection > Select highlighted cylindrical face to apply new constraint > Specify **Slot–Pivot** for Name.

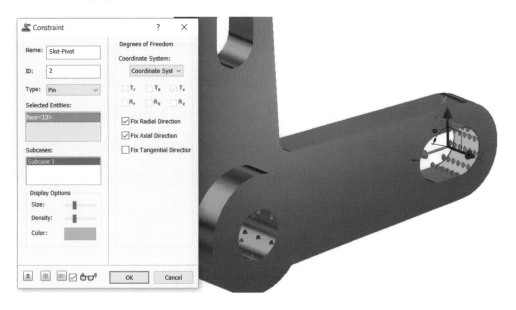

9. Click **OK** > Select **Loads** > Specify **Pin-Load** for Name > Select **Bearing Load** for Load Type > Select **Components** for Direction > Select highlighted cylindrical face to apply load > Specify **-30** for Magnitude (N) in Fx field > **Select Preview** so you can adjust display options as desired.

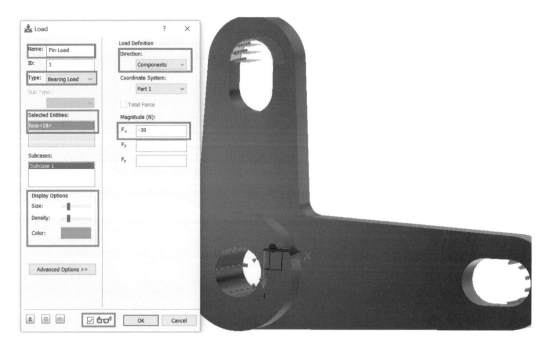

10. Click **OK** > Select **Mesh Settings** > Specify **2** for Element Size (mm).

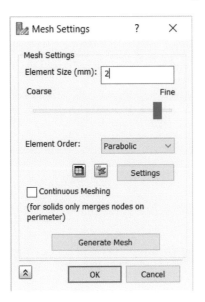

11. Click **OK**.

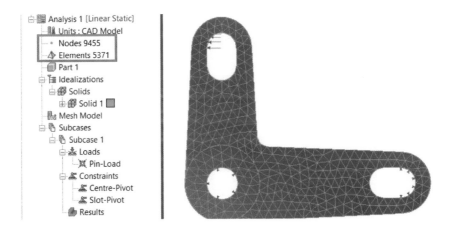

A total of 5371 tetrahedral elements will be generated.

CHAPTER 2

DP1 – Part Analysis – Lever Arm

Run simulation and analyse

12. Select **Run** > Click **OK** when run is complete > Select **Object Visibility** > Unselect **Undeformed Edges**.

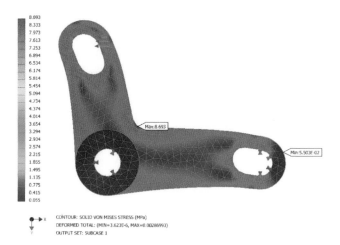

During the run you will get several warnings. These warnings are referring to the tetrahedral element warnings. These warnings can be reduced by further refining the mesh.

The maximum von Mises stress is 8.693MPa giving us a factor of safety of 23.

$$Factor\ of\ Safety = \frac{200}{8.693} = 23$$

This suggests our design is considerably over-engineered meaning we can further optimise the design. Before this we need to check whether the stress value is not mesh sensitive. In other words, we need to investigate whether the stress value does not change by altering the mesh size.

13. Right click **Analysis 1** > Select **Duplicate**. This will duplicate idealizations, loads, and constraints.

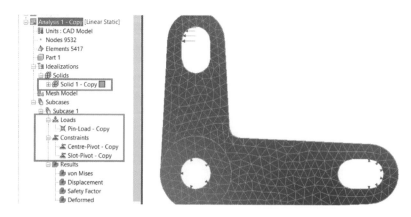

An alternative method is to create a new analysis and then drag and drop boundary conditions and other settings from the model tree to the analysis tree.

14.   Select **Mesh Settings** > Specify **1** for Element Size (mm) > Click **OK**.

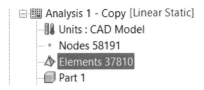

This will create 37810 elements. This is more than 7 times the first analysis. So, reducing the mesh by half does not necessarily produce twice as much elements.

15.   Select **Run** again > Click **OK** when run is complete.

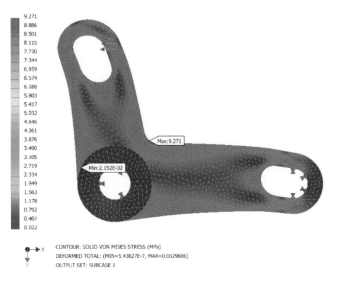

The maximum von Mises stress has increased to 9.271N that is about 6.6% increase in value. We will run the analysis again and see if this percentage increase reduces.

16.   Select **New** Analysis from the Nastran In-CAD panel > Click **OK**.

17.   Select **Solid1** Idealization > Keeping **left mouse button pressed** drag the **Solid1** idealization onto the Idealizations node in the new Analysis 3 > Now **release left mouse button**. This will copy Solid1 idealization.

18.   Repeat step 16 to copy **Centre-Pivot** constraint, **Slot-Pivot** constraint and **Pin-Load**. Making sure to release left mouse button on the Constraints node for constraints and Loads node for loads.

CHAPTER 2

DP1 – Part Analysis – Lever Arm

Now rather than changing the global mesh size we will define a local mesh control in the high stress area. The benefit of this method is that it will not generate excessive elements in low stress areas.

19. Select **Mesh Control** > Select Face Data option by clicking in the Selected Faces box > Specify **0.5** for Element Size (mm) > Select the highlighted face.

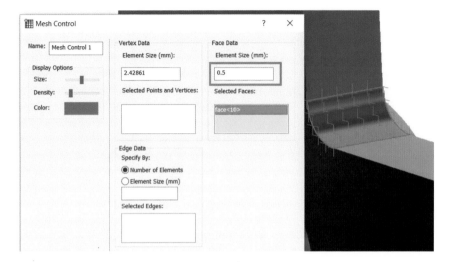

20. Click **OK** > Select **Mesh Settings** > Specify **1** for Element Size (mm) > Select **Settings** to access Advanced Mesh Settings > Specify **1.1** for Max Element Growth Rate.

21. Click **OK** twice > Select **Run** > Click **OK** when run is complete.

22. Unselect **Deformed** from the Results panel to see undeformed plot.

23. Select **Object Visibility** > Unselect **Mesh Controls**. This will hide symbols for mesh control.

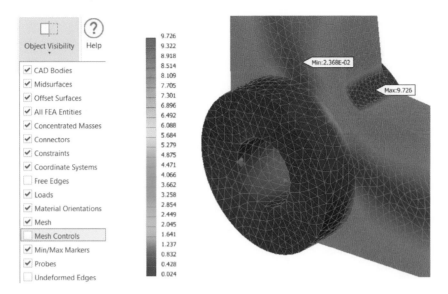

The maximum von Mises stress has now increased to 9.726N which is about 5% increase in value. The percentage change in maximum von Mises stress value has reduced and suggests the values will eventually converge by further mesh refinement. At this stage we can take this value to calculate our factor of safety or we can alternatively run one more simulation with a finer local mesh. We will use the latter option.

24. Right click **Mesh Control 1** > Select **Edit** > Specify **0.25** for Element Size > Click **OK** > Select **Generate Mesh**.

25. Select **Run** > Click **OK** when run is complete.

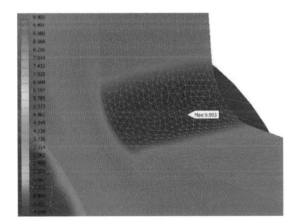

The maximum von Mises stress has increased to 9.903N which is about 1.5% increase in value. So, we can confidentially say the results have converged. We have a factor of safety value of 20.

$$Factor\ of\ Safety = \frac{200}{9.903} = 20$$

We can also plot Safety Factor plots in Inventor Nastran.

26. Double click **Safety Factor** results plot. To better visualise and understand safety factor results we can modify the colour legend scale.

27. Right click on **Safety Factor** Plot in browser > Select **Edit** > Select **Specify Min/Max** > Specify **100** for Data Max > Unselect **Deform Options** > Select **Display**.

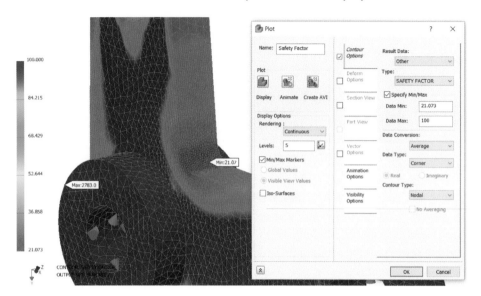

The minimum safety factor, in same location, is 21.07 slightly higher than the previously calculated value. So, the question is why are the values different? The answer is that the calculated stress value is based on the average stress value at the node location. Whereas the safety factor plot values are based on taking the average of the nodal safety factors. This can be best explained by the following example. We will use 200MPa for yield limit for comparison purposes.

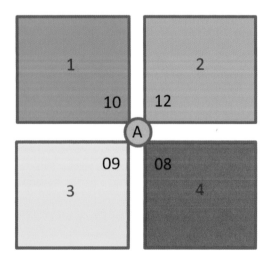

Safety factor calculation based on average stress at location A is 20.51.

Average Stress value = (10+12+9+8)/4 = 9.75

Safety Factor = 200/9.75 = 20.51

Safety factor calculation based on how Inventor Nastran displays plots at Location A is 20.97.

Safety Factor for Element 1 = 200/10 = 20

Safety Factor for Element 2 = 200/12 = 16.667

Safety Factor for Element 3 = 200/9 = 22.222

Safety Factor for Element 4 = 200/8 = 25

Average Safety Factor = (20+16.667+22.222+25)/4 = 20.97

So, this is the reason why there is a slight difference in the safety factor results. Both results are correct as they have been calculated in slightly different ways. It is entirely up to yourself which value you take.

For comparison purposes changing the data type display to centroidal results changes the von mises stress value to 9.454MPa.

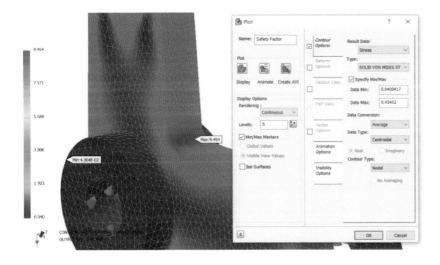

So, based on this value the factor of safety now becomes 21.15.

$$Factor\ of\ Safety = \frac{200}{9.454} = 21.15$$

This is very close to the Safety Factor plot value of 21.07 with a difference of less than 0.5%.

Use average centroidal stress values when comparing with safety factor plots.

CHAPTER 2
DP1 – Part Analysis – Lever Arm

Redesign – Reduce weight

As the factor of safety of 21.15 is well above 5 we can alter the design considerably. Here is one redesign example you could consider or perhaps you could come up with your own innovative design.

CONTOUR: SOLID VON MISES STRESS (MPa)
OUTPUT SET: SUBCASE 2

The Nastran In-CAD Safety Factor plot value of 6.103 is the same as the calculated value of 6.12, based on the average centroidal stress result.

$$Factor\ of\ Safety = \frac{200}{32.648} = 6.12$$

So, we can now consider this optimised redesign fit for purpose.

28. Close File.

DP2 – Part Analysis – Prop Shaft Yoke

(Design problem courtesy of GKN Land Systems)

Key features and workflows introduced in this design problem

	Key Features/Workflows
1	**Fixed Constraint**
2	**Moment Load**
3	**Rigid Body Connector**
4	**Advanced Mesh Settings**
5	**Global and Local Face Mesh Control**
6	**Nodal and Centroidal Results**
7	**Stress Singularities**
8	**Section View Plot**

Introduction

GKN Motorsport is a sub-sector of GKN Land Systems and manufactures driveshafts, prop shafts and CV joints for applications such as world rally and touring cars. This also includes driveline components and assemblies for high performance road cars. Motorsport parts are often highly stressed; however, weight is also an important aspect, and parts must be lightweight, without compromising performance.

In this design problem we are going to analyse a high strength yoke used on a WRC prop shaft using the following design information and goal.

Design Information

Material of Lever - **Steel 300M**
Density - **7850kg/m³**
Youngs Modulus - **207GPa**
Poisson's Ratio - **0.33**
Yield Limit - **1550MPa**
Moment Load - **3000Nm**
Minimum Safety Factor - **1**

Design Goal
Stress does not exceed yield limit.

Workflow of Design Problem 2

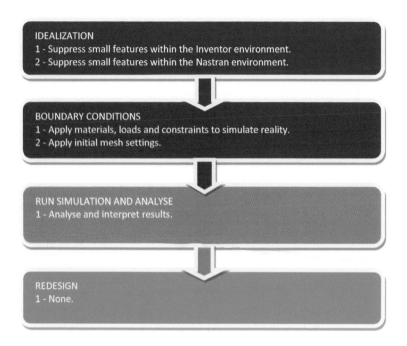

Idealization

We are going to suppress some non-structural features using Inventor's Direct Edit tool.

1.   Open *Female Rear yoke.ipt*

2.   Move **End of Part** below Direct Edit3 feature.

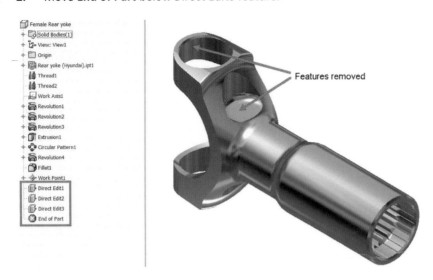

This will remove the hole and groove features in the yoke. The other small features around the teeth of the yoke will be suppressed using Inventor Nastran mesh settings.

Boundary conditions

3.   Select **Environments** tab > Select **Autodesk Inventor Nastran**.

As it stands there is no appropriate geometrical entity on the yoke to which we can apply a moment load to. At this stage we have two options.

- Include the load transmitting components and perform an assembly analysis including contacts etc.
- Create a rigid body connector – this is basically a simplified representation of a very stiff (or strong) component.

In this design problem we are going to use the latter option.

4. Select **Connectors** from the Prepare panel > Select **Rigid Body** from Connector Type > Select the two highlighted faces for Dependent Entities > Click in the Select Point selection box > Select **Work point <1>** for Independent Vertex/Point > Adjust the display options as desired.

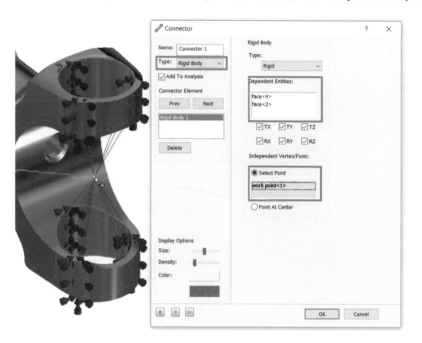

5. Click **OK** > Select **Constraints** > Select face on one side of tooth and then continue for the remaining teeth.

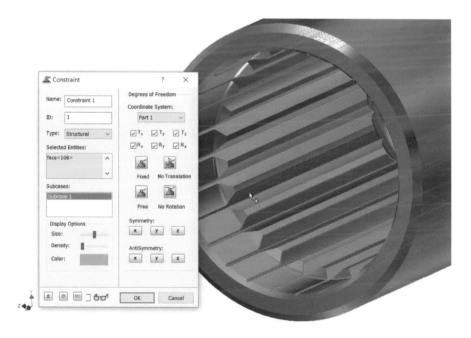

Fixed constraint is selected by default.

6.   Click **OK** > Select **Loads** > Select **Moment** for Load Type > Select **Components** for Direction, if not already selected > Specify **3000 N m** for Magnitude in Fx field > Select **work point <1>** > Select **Preview** to display load symbol.

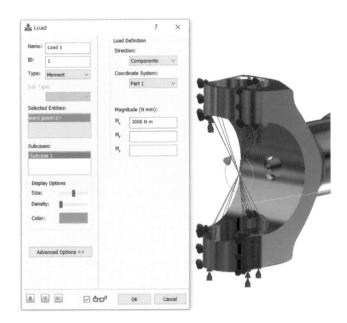

✏️ Specifying 3000 N m will convert the value to 3,000,000Nmm, as default units are in Nmm.

7.   Click **OK** > Select **Mesh Settings** > Specify **3** for Element Size (mm) > Click **OK**.

This mesh size together with default settings will try to include small features along the entire length of teeth, as illustrated below.

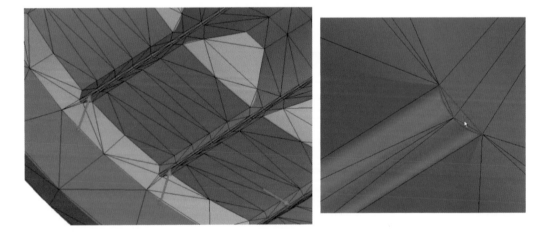

Typically, such features will be suppressed within the modelling environment. But here we will use the advance mesh settings to exclude small features from mesh generation.

8. Select **Mesh Settings** > Select **Settings** to access Advanced Mesh Settings > Specify **20** for Suppress Short Features > **Select** Project Midside Nodes > Specify **1.1** for Max Element Growth Rate.

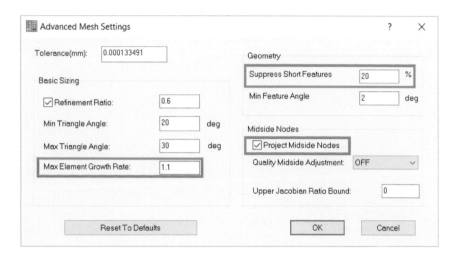

Project Midside Nodes will project the middle node of the elements onto curved geometry. Thus, helping to better represent geometry with high curvatures.

9. Click **OK** twice. This will regenerate mesh.

10. Select **Object Visibility** > Unselect **CAD Bodies** > Unselect **Constraints** > Unselect **Loads**.

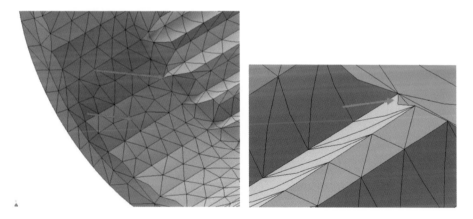

Hiding the CAD body will help to interrogate the mesh more easily.

We can clearly see the small features are now not included in the mesh. These small features if included can cause high stresses, also referred to as hot spots and stress singularities.

11. Select **Object Visibility** > Reselect **CAD Bodies**.

Run simulation and analyse

12. Select **Run** > Click **OK** when run is complete.

13. Select **Object Visibility** > Unselect **Undeformed Edges** > Unselect **Connectors**.

📝 You may need to reselect and then unselect All FEA entities.

14. Select **Displacement** plot. Maximum displacement is 1.013mm.

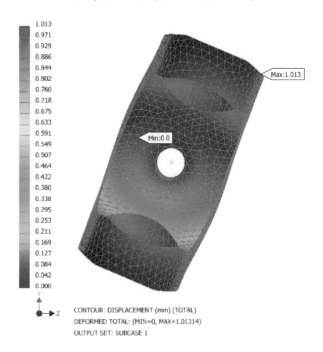

15. Select **Animate** from the Results panel.

16. Deselect **Animate** to stop animation after viewing the results.

17. Right click **von Mises** plot in the browser > Select **Edit** > Change Name to **von Mises Centroidal Average** > Unselect **Deform Options** > Select **Centroidal** for Data Type > Select **Display**.

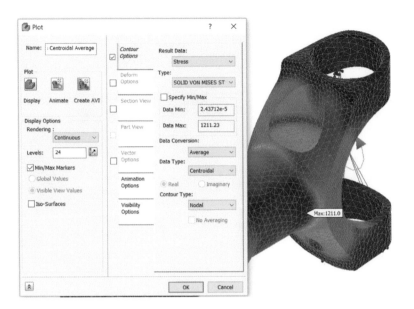

Maximum von Mises stress is 1211MPa.

Centroidal results take the average centroidal stresses of all attached elements.

18. Click **OK** > Right click **Safety Factor** plot in the browser > Select **Edit** > Unselect **Deform Options** > Select **Specify Min/Max** > Specify **15** for Data Max > Select **Display**.

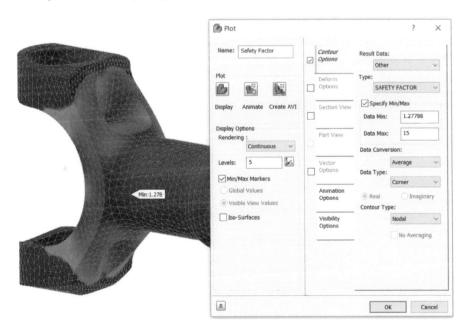

CHAPTER 3

DP2 – Part Analysis – Prop Shaft Yoke

Based on average centroidal stress the calculated F.O.S is 1.28 which same as Inventor Nastran Safety Factor plot.

$$Factor\ of\ Safety = \frac{1550}{1211} = 1.28$$

Below is a tabular result of all the von Mises stress options.

Data Type	Data Conversion	Location	Value (MPa)
Maximum	Corner	Near teeth	1965
Minimum	Corner		1354
Average	Corner	On radius of product	1395
Maximum	Centroidal		1314
Minimum	Centroidal		1128
Average	Centroidal		1211

Maximum nodal value is probably a stress singularity due to sharp edges/points as all other values are at the radius of the yoke.

The percentage difference between the minimum and maximum centroidal results is between 14% and 17%. Plus, the difference between corner minimum and average values is 3%. Further the difference between the average results is 13%. We can further reduce the difference between the average corner and average centroidal results by further refining the mesh, in area of high stress.

At this stage we have two options

    a.   Take the maximum value 1395MPa at the radius of the yoke as basis for safety factor calculations.

    b.   Reduce the mesh size around the radius of the yoke and check the difference in the centroidal results.

We will use both options.

Using option a we have a factor of safety value of 1.11.

$$Factor\ of\ Safety = \frac{1550}{1395} = 1.11$$

The following steps are to determine option b.

19. Select **Return** > Select **Mesh Control** > Select Face Data option by clicking in the Selected Faces box > Specify **1** for Element Size (mm) > Select the highlighted face.

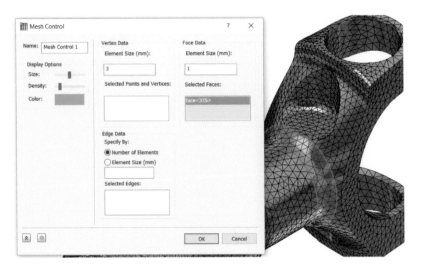

20. Click **OK** > Select **Generate Mesh**.

21. Click **OK** > Select **Run** > Click **OK** once run is complete.

22. Select **Object Visibility** > Unselect **Mesh Control** > Select **von Mises Centroidal Average** plot.

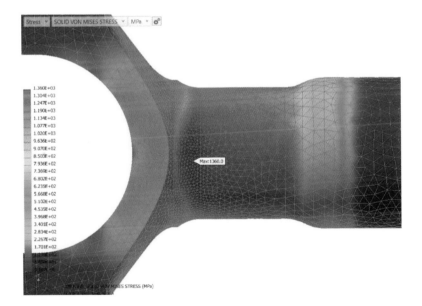

The maximum stress value is 1360MPa. This is within 4% of 1414MPa (new average corner stress).

Now we will have a look at the stress around the teeth.

23. Click **OK** > Right Click **Results** > Select **New** > Specify **Section View** for Name > Select **Maximum** for Data Conversion > Select **Corner** for Data Type.

24. Select **Section View** > Unselect **Deform Options** > Select **Section with Cut Solid** > Flip direction of cut only if it does not show maximum stress value.

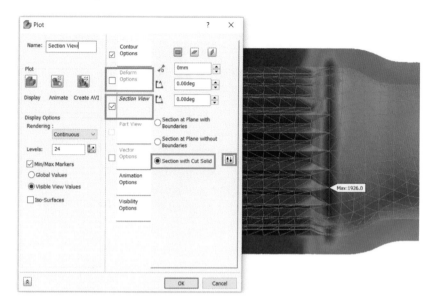

This max stress is most likely caused by stress singularities due to sharp edges. Although this shows a lot higher stress than the radius area we can investigate the stress around the area of interest.

To find the maximum nodal stress around the radius area we can make use of fringe results and modify maximum value of the stress on the legend bar. The maximum value can be altered until you get a minimum amount of grey contour around the radius area. This will then make it easier to place probe at the point of high stress in area of interest.

25. Unselect **Section View** > Select **Contour Options** > Select **Fringe** for Rendering options > Select **Specify Min/Max** > Specify **1410** for Data Max > Select **Display**.

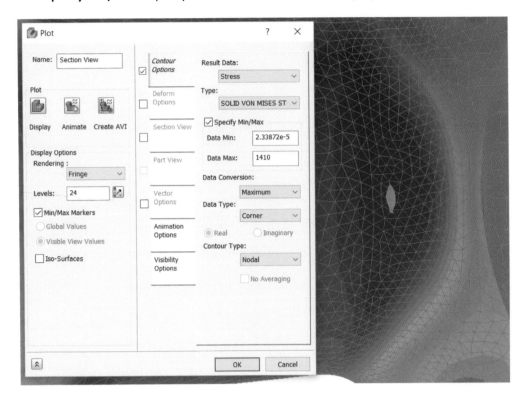

26. Click **OK** > Select **Probes** from the Results panel > Move the probe around the grey area to get a feel for the values > Click to place probe at maximum value location.

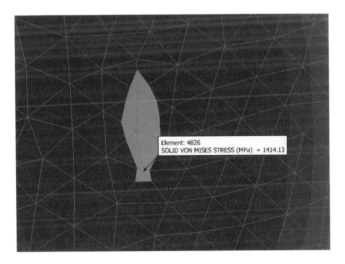

27. Deselect **Probes.**

So, in summary we have the following values at the radius area:

Average Centroidal   = 1360MPa

Average Corner   = 1414MPa

Max Nodal in area of interest   = 1414MPa

All these results are within 4% difference. As a rule of thumb in the FEA world a value of 10% is typically used as a basis for result convergence. So, taking the higher value the factor of safety is now 1.096.

$$Factor\ of\ Safety = \frac{1550}{1414} = 1.096$$

As the result is above 1 we can confidently say the design is fit for purpose.

Other ways to rule out stress singularities or stresses above yield value are;

- To plot a section view across the high stress point and then check how much of the high stress is penetrating through thickness.
- To run a non-linear analysis to check for any localised yielding and true stress values.

28. Close File.

DP3 – Assembly Analysis – Lever

(Design Problem courtesy of Magnet Schultz Limited)

Key features and workflows introduced in this design problem

	Key Features/Workflows
1	Fixed Constraint
2	Frictionless Constraint
3	Bearing Load
4	Symmetry Conditions
5	Automatic Contacts
6	Advanced Mesh Settings
7	Global and Local Face Mesh Control
8	Display full model results from a half symmetry model

Introduction

Magnet Schultz Ltd are the leading solenoid specialists in UK since 1967 and have high profile customers in a variety of industries including defence, automotive and security. Typical products designed include the T61 Right-angle Solenoid Shot bolt as illustrated below.

In this design problem we are going to analyse the lever as an assembly using the following design information and goal.

Design Information

Lever
Material of Lever - **Steel**
Density - **7850kg/m³**
Youngs Modulus - **200GPa**
Poisson's Ratio - **0.29**
Yield Limit - **200MPa**
Load - **30N**
Minimum Safety Factor - **5**

Pins
Material of Lever - **Steel Alloy**
Density - **7730kg/m³**
Youngs Modulus - **205GPa**
Poisson's Ratio - **0.3**
Yield Limit - **250MPa**
Load - **30N**
Minimum Safety Factor - **5**

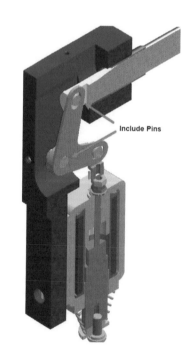

Include Pins

Design Goal

Is to reanalyse the original lever design as an assembly analysis.

Workflow of Design Problem 3

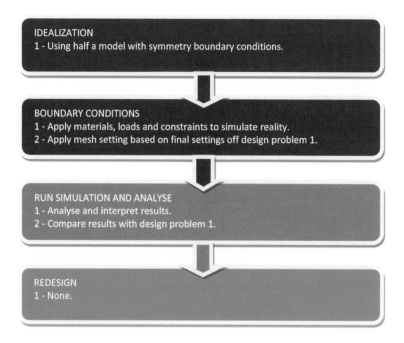

IDEALIZATION
1 - Using half a model with symmetry boundary conditions.

BOUNDARY CONDITIONS
1 - Apply materials, loads and constraints to simulate reality.
2 - Apply mesh setting based on final settings off design problem 1.

RUN SIMULATION AND ANALYSE
1 - Analyse and interpret results.
2 - Compare results with design problem 1.

REDESIGN
1 - None.

Idealization

We are going to analyse half of the assembly using symmetry conditions. This is standard procedure when both geometry and loading are symmetrical. With the added advantage of reducing the file size by at least half with faster run times.

1.   Open *Lever-Assembly.iam*

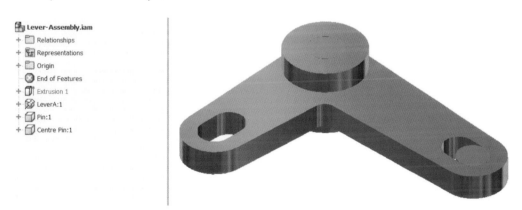

Lever-Assembly.iam
+ ☐ Relationships
+ ☐ Representations
+ ☐ Origin
+ ⊗ End of Features
+ ☐ Extrusion 1
+ ☐ LeverA:1
+ ☐ Pin:1
+ ☐ Centre Pin:1

2. Move **End of Features** below **Extrusion 1**.

Extrusion 1 is defined in the assembly environment as it is easier to half all parts in one extrusion when compared to extruding in part environment for each component. The other advantage of this method is, it does not alter the original parts.

Boundary conditions

3. Select **Environments** tab > Select **Autodesk Inventor Nastran**.

Materials for the lever (similar to design problem 1) and pins are already defined.

4. Select **Constraints** > Specify **Fixed Constraints** for Name > Select highlighted faces of both pins to apply constraint > Select **Preview** so you can adjust display options as desired.

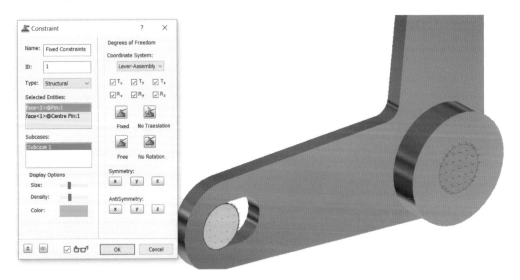

5. Click **OK**.

6. Select **Frictionless Constraints** > Select all 3 highlighted faces to apply new constraint > Specify **Z-Symmetry** for Name > Select **Preview** so you can adjust display options as desired.

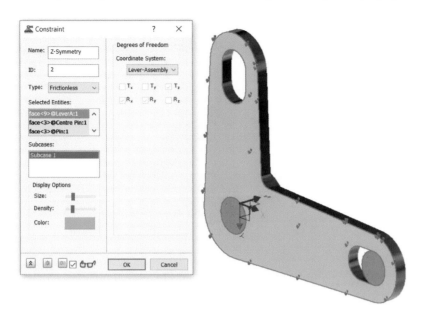

💡 Frictionless constraints are commonly used to specify symmetry conditions.

7. Click **OK** > Select **Loads** > Specify **Pin-Load** for Name > Select **Bearing Load** for Load Type > Select highlighted face to apply load > Select **Components** for Direction > Specify **-15** for Magnitude in Fx field > **Select Preview** so you can adjust display options as desired.

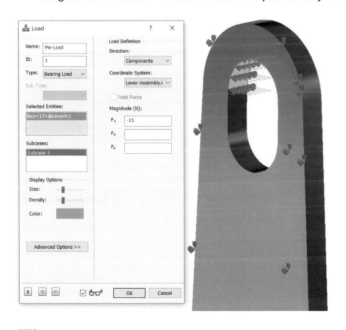

📝 15N is specified as we are using half a model.

8.   Click **OK** > Select **Mesh Control** > Select Face Data option by clicking in the Selected Faces box > Specify **0.25** for Element Size (mm) > Select the highlighted face.

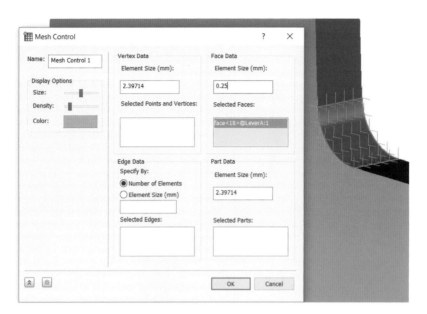

9.   Click **OK** > Select **Mesh Settings** > Specify **1** for Element Size (mm) > Select **Settings** to access Advanced Mesh Settings > Specify **1.1** for Max Element Growth Rate > Click **OK twice**.

These mesh settings are same as the final mesh settings for the lever example in design problem 1.

10.   Select **Automatic** contacts from the Contacts panel.

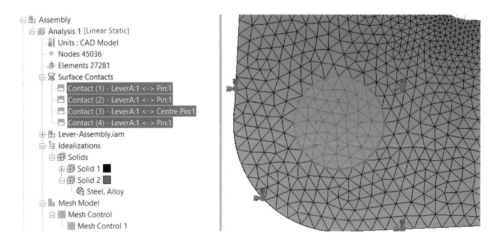

This will create 4 bonded contacts between lever and the two pins. Pins in reality are not bonded and instead allow rotation and possible separation from the lever when a high enough load is applied.

11. Right click selected contacts > Select **Edit** > Select **Separation** for Contact Type.

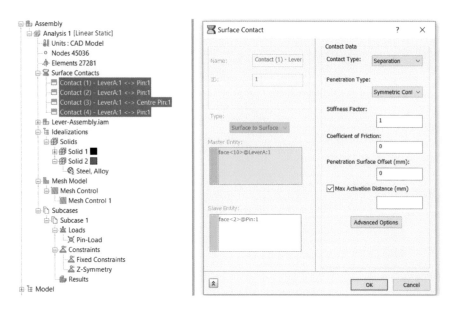

12. Click **OK** > Select **Contacts (1) & (4)** > Right click selected contacts > Select **Suppress**

This suppresses the contacts that are created between the flat faces of the slot and the pin.

🖊 The contact numbering maybe different so take care in suppressing contacts.

CHAPTER 4

DP3 – Assembly Analysis – Lever

Run simulation and analyse

13. Select **Run** > Click **OK** once run is complete.

14. Select **Object Visibility** > Unselect **All FEA Entities** > Reselect **Mesh**

You may need to reselect and then unselect All FEA entities again

15. Unselect **Deformed** from the Results panel.

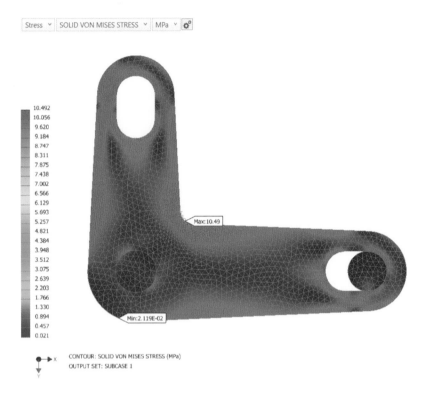

The maximum stress (nodal average based) is 10.49MPa.

16. Select **Displacement** results > Unselect **Deformed** from the Results panel if not already selected.

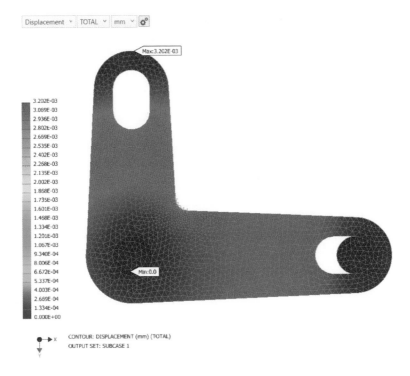

Maximum displacement is 0.003202mm

The maximum stress and displacement for the lever when analysed as a single part are;

- von Mises (nodal average based) is 9.903MPa
- Max displacement is 0.00296mm

The percentage difference between the stress results is below 6%. So why is there a difference in the results? Should you analyse as a single part or as assembly? Let's take a closer look.

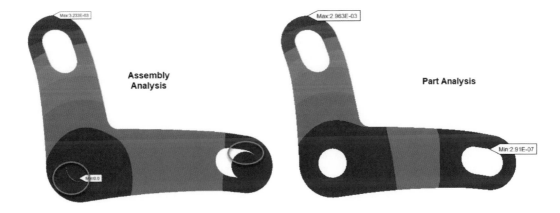

CHAPTER 4

DP3 – Assembly Analysis – Lever

We can see that the assembly analysis shows more movement which is due to the separation contacts allowing the lever to separate from pins, like reality. This behaviour cannot be simulated in part analysis. The extra movement in the assembly will result in a higher stress than the part analysis.

As the difference between both analyses is not significant it is entirely down to you of which method you prefer. It is also good practice to start from part analysis to get a good idea of part behaviour and then move onto assembly analysis to get a more realistic analysis.

Since we analysed a half model we can use ground planes to display full model results.

17. Select **Object Visibility** > > Unselect **Mesh** > Unselect **Min/Max Marker**.

18. Right click **von Mises stress** results > Select **Edit** > Select **Specify Min/Max** > Specify **0** for Data Min and **5** Data Max > Select **Display** > Click **OK**.

19. Change the view of the model using cube as shown below.

20. Select View tab > Click on **Ground Plane** icon to display plane

21. Right click cube > Select **Set Current View** as **Front**.

Ground Plane

22. Click on **Reflections** icon to display reflection.

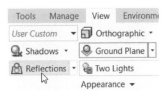

23. Select **Reflection Settings**.

24. Change the Reflection Settings as shown below.

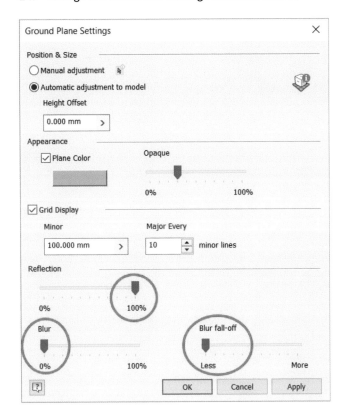

Reflection	**100%**
Blur	**0%**
Blur fall-off	**Less**

25. Click **OK**.

26. Click on **Ground Plane** icon to hide plane > Move the model slightly until you see the reflection as shown below. This gives the impression the full model was analysed.

Below are Displacement results.

27. Close File, after viewing and analysing results.

DP4 – Assembly Analysis – Bolted Bridge Structure

(Design Problem courtesy of Canal & River Trust)

Key features and workflows introduced in this design problem

	Key Features/Workflows
1	**Fixed Constraints**
2	**Frictionless Constraints**
3	**Symmetry Conditions**
4	**Bolt Connectors**
5	**Manual Contacts**
6	**Global and Local Face Mesh Control**
7	**Part Mesh Control**
8	**Bolts Results Processing**

CHAPTER 5
DP4 – Bolted Assembly Analysis – Bolted Bridge Structure

Introduction

The types and sizes of bridges on Britain's canals are almost as numerous as the bridges themselves, and many are manually operated. As part of an ongoing programme of safety improvements, these bridges are being modified to allow them to be operated from either side of the canal and to provide restraint to a large moving mass. The visual impact of any modifications must be minimised due to the heritage value of the canals, which is closely regulated. The method chosen for opening/closing the bridge is a hydraulic cylinder (jack), which is to be placed underneath the bridge deck. To accommodate the jack a new structure will be required. This structure will be placed between the new jack and the existing structure underneath the bridge.

In this design problem we are going to analyse the new structure and the bolts required to attach the new structure using the following design information and goal.

Design Information

Main Structure
Material - **Mild Steel**
Youngs Modulus - **220GPa**
Yield Limit - **207MPa**
Poisson's Ratio - **0.275**
Bearing Load - **30,000N**
Minimum F.O.S - **4**

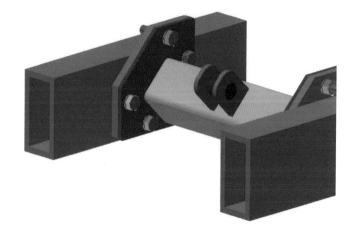

Bolts
Material - **Steel Galvanised**
Youngs Modulus - **250GPa**
Yield Limit - **300MPa**
Poisson's Ratio - **0.3**
Bearing Load - **30,000N**
Minimum F.O.S – **2.5**
Bolt Size minimum **M18**

Design Goal
Stress meets minimum F.O.S criteria.

Workflow of Design Problem 4

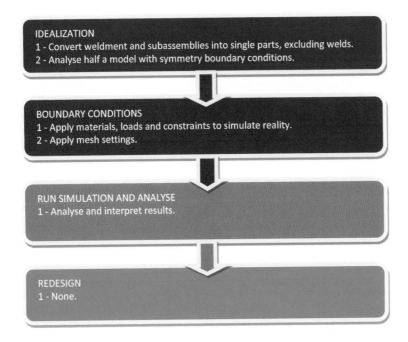

IDEALIZATION
1 - Convert weldment and subassemblies into single parts, excluding welds.
2 - Analyse half a model with symmetry boundary conditions.

BOUNDARY CONDITIONS
1 - Apply materials, loads and constraints to simulate reality.
2 - Apply mesh settings.

RUN SIMULATION AND ANALYSE
1 - Analyse and interpret results.

REDESIGN
1 - None.

Idealization

The material property of the main bridge structure and the new structure are being manufactured from the same material, mild steel. In addition, both the bridge structure and the new structure are welded. Therefore, for simplicity the assembly can be shrink-wrapped or derived into separate parts as illustrated below. The additional benefit of this will be a reduced number of contacts required.

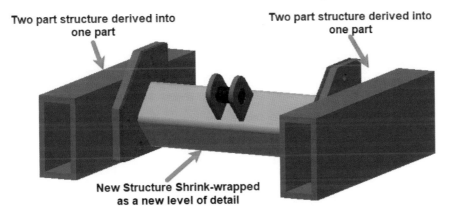

Two part structure derived into one part

Two part structure derived into one part

New Structure Shrink-wrapped as a new level of detail

CHAPTER 5
DP4 – Bolted Assembly Analysis – Bolted Bridge Structure

1.   Open *Bolt-Analysis.iam*

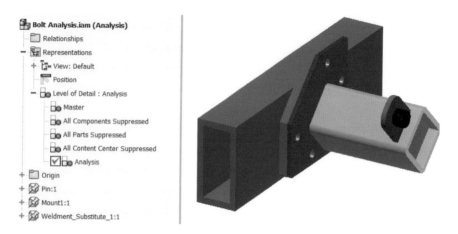

Boundary conditions

2.   Select **Environments** tab > Select **Autodesk Inventor Nastran**.

3.   Right click **Pin:1** > Select **Exclude from Analysis**.

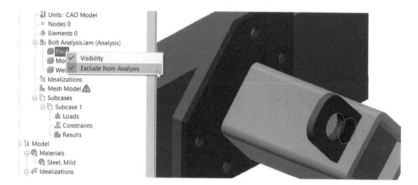

This simplifies the analysis further by reducing the number of parts and contacts needed to analyse the assembly. Plus, more importantly we are not interested in the analysis of the pin. Instead we will apply a bearing load to represent load exerted by pin onto the structure.

4. Select **Loads** > Specify **Pin-Load** for Name > Select **Bearing Load** for Load Type > Select the highlighted face for Selected Entities > Select **Components** for Direction > Specify **-15000** for Magnitude in Fx field > **Select Preview** so you can adjust display options as desired.

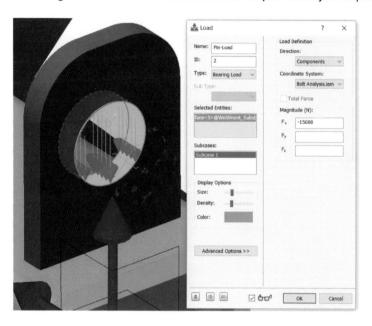

5. Click **OK** > Select **Constraints** > Specify **Fixed Constraints** for Name > Select the two highlighted faces of existing bridge structure to apply constraints > Select **Preview** so you can adjust display options as desired.

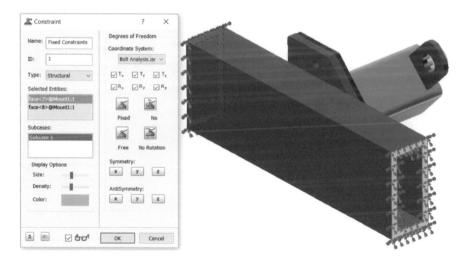

6. Click **OK**.

7. Select **Frictionless Constraints** > Select highlighted face > Select **Preview** so you can adjust display options as desired.

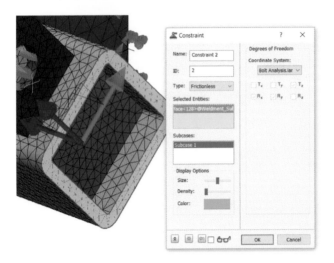

8. Click **OK** > Right Click **Solid 1** > Select **Edit** > Delete **Pin:1** from Selected Entities > Change **Color** of mesh to **black**.

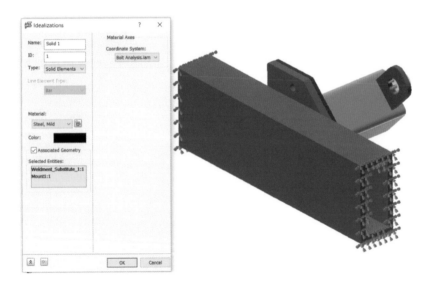

9. Click **OK** twice > Select **Generate Mesh** to get an idea of the mesh size > Click **OK**.

10. Select **Local Mesh** control > Select Part Data option by clicking in the Selected Parts box > Specify **10** for Element Size (mm) > Select **Weldment_Substitute_1:1** part.

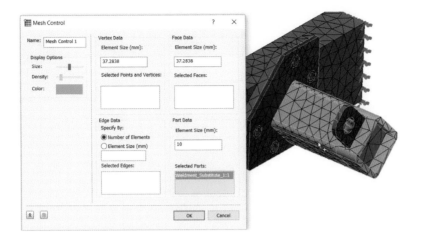

11. Click **OK** > Select **Mesh Settings** > Specify **20** for Element Size (mm) > Select **Settings** to access Advanced Mesh Settings > Specify **1.1** for Max Element Growth Rate > Select **Project Midside Nodes** > Click **OK** twice.

12. Select **Manual** contacts from the Contacts panel.

13. Select **face** of Mount1:1 as shown for Master Entity.

14. Click in the Slave Entity selection box > Select **face** of Weldment_Substitute_1:1 in contact with Mount1:1.

15. Click OK.

Now we need to create bolt and cap screw connections to hold the structure together.

16. Select **Connectors** from the Prepare panel > Select **Bolt** from Connector Type > Select **Torque** for Preload > Specify **16000** for Preload (N mm) > Specify **0.2** for Torque Coefficient > Select **User Defined** for Materials > Specify **250000** for Youngs Modulus > Specify **0.3** for Poisson's Ratio.

The formula used to calculate preload based on torque option is,

$$Preload = \frac{Torque}{Torque\ Coeficient * Bolt\ Diameter}$$

Where torque coefficient can be found in standard engineering textbooks. Below are some values.

Bolt Conditions	Coefficient
Non-Plated	0.3
Zinc-Plate	0.2
Cadmium-Plate	0.16

17. Select the split face as shown for Bearing surface for bolt head.

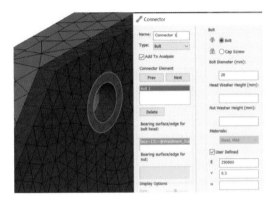

As soon as you pick the split face Inventor Nastran will populate the bolt diameter value field with a size based on the diameter of the hole.

If a split surface is not created the bolt connection will create a rigid connection based on selecting the edge of the hole, resulting in high stresses. It is therefore best practice to always create a split face to represent the bolt head (and nut) load bearing face.

18. Select the split face on the other end for Bearing surface for nut.

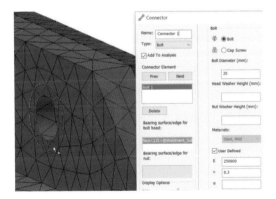

CHAPTER 5

DP4 – Bolted Assembly Analysis – Bolted Bridge Structure

19. Select **3** for Head Washer Height (mm) > Select **3** for Nut Washer Height (mm). A bolt connector will be created as shown below.

Below is an image (not to scale) of how Nastran In-CAD represents a bolted connection.

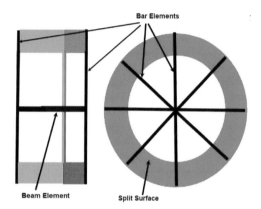

The main shank of the bolt is represented by a beam element with the same sectional properties of the bolt. Whereas the bar elements cross sectional properties are based on a half diameter of the bolt with the same material properties as the bolt.

 Adding the washers increases the effective length of the beam element by the same amount as washer heights. This will thus represent the bolt more accurately.

20. Specify **18** for Bolt Diameter (mm).

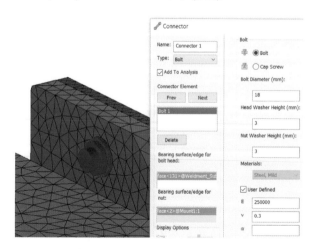

The next 3 connectors will be created using cap screw for the ease of installing onsite.

21. Click **OK** > Select **Connectors** again > Select **Bolt** from Connector Type > Select **Cap Screw** option > Select **Torque** for Preload > Specify **16000** for Preload (N mm) > Specify **0.2** for Torque Coefficient > Select **User Defined** for Materials > Specify **250000** for Youngs Modulus > Specify **0.3** for Poisson's Ratio > Select split surface for Bearing surface for bolt head > Select internal hole of the other part for Surface for threaded region > Select **3** for Head Washer Height.

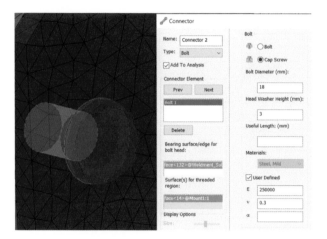

22. Select **Next** and continue creating two more cap screw connectors > Specify **18** for Bolt Diameter (mm).

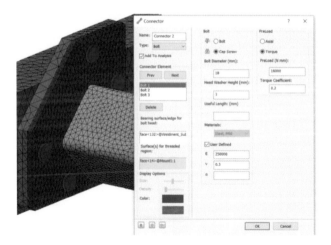

CHAPTER 5

DP4 – Bolted Assembly Analysis – Bolted Bridge Structure

Below is an image (not to scale) of how Nastran In-CAD represents caps screws.

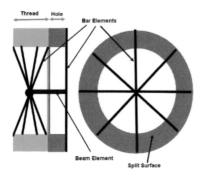

L = Length of effective beam element.

LHole = Length of hole.

If "Useful Length" is blank, the length of the beam element representing the body of the bolt (L) is equal to

$$L = LHole + 0.5 * d$$

Where
d = bolt diameter.

 Useful Length is used in situations where the geometry representing the bolt is not accurate. If specified this value will be taken as the new L value.

23. Click **OK**.

We are now going to create local mesh control on the connector split faces as these will be the high stress regions.

 Hide the connectors to be able to select split surfaces with ease.

24. Select **Mesh Control** > Select Face Data option by clicking in the Selected Faces box > Specify **4** for Element Size (mm) > Select all five split faces.

25. Click **OK** > Select **Generate Mesh**.

26. Right Click **Analysis 1** > Select **Edit** > Select **Force** from Output Sets.

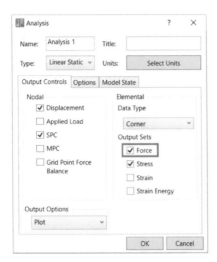

This output is required to determine forces in the bolts.

Run simulation and analyse

27. Select **Run** > Click **OK** > Select **Animate** from the Results panel.

28. Unselect **Animate**, after analysing the results > Unselect **Deformed** > Select **Object Visibility** > Unselect **Constraints** > Unselect **Loads** > Unselect **Mesh Controls**.

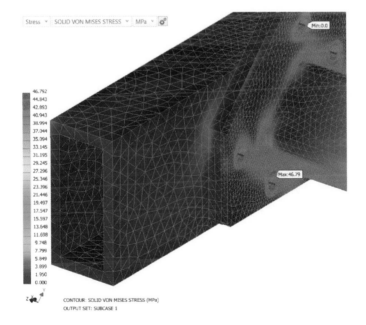

CHAPTER 5
DP4 – Bolted Assembly Analysis – Bolted Bridge Structure

The maximum stress is 46.8MPa (based on nodal average results). This gives us a factor of safety value of 4.4.

$$Factor\ of\ Safety = \frac{207}{46.8} = 4.4$$

This meets our minimum value of 4. Now let's check the stress in the bolts.

29. Select **Beam von Mises stress from** the results navigation bar within the graphic window.

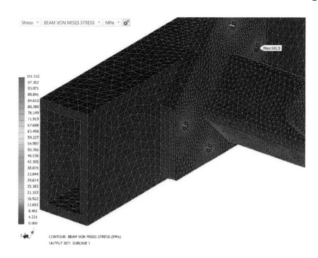

The maximum stress in the beam is 101.5MPa giving a safety factor value off 2.95.

$$Factor\ of\ Safety = \frac{300}{101.5} = 2.95$$

Now we will have a look at the forces in the beams.

30. Select **Beam Diagram** > Select **Beam Force End A-X**.

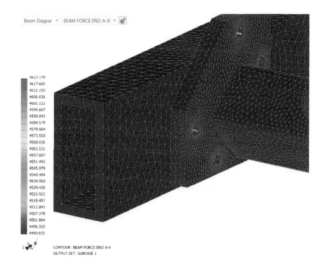

The maximum axial force in the beam is 4623N.

Below is an explanation of some common beam results.

Type	Result
Beam Force End A-X	Axial Force
Beam Force End A-Y Plane 1	Shear Force in the local Y direction
Beam Force End A-Z Plane 2	Shear Force in the local Z direction
Beam Moment End A-X	Torsion in the bolt due to rotation
Beam Moment End A-Y Plane 1	Moment about the local Y direction
Beam Moment End A-Z Plane 2	Moment about the local Z direction

End A and End B are the ends of the beam element as shown below.

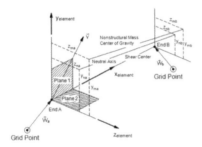

(image captured from Autodesk online help)

31. Select **Beam Force End A-Y Plane 1**.

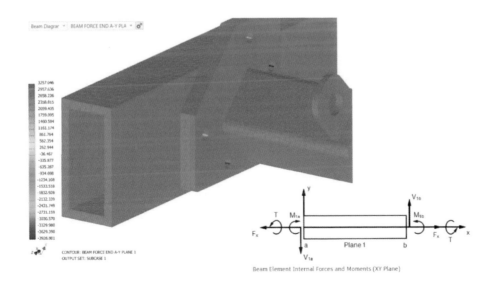

The maximum shear force in the local Y direction in the beam is 3257N.

32. Select **Beam Force End A-Z Plane 2**.

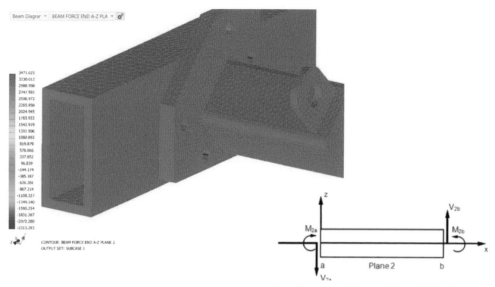

Beam Element Internal Forces and Moments (XZ Plane)

The maximum shear force in the local Z direction in the beam is 3471N.

Total shear force (resultant) can be calculated from shear force in Y and Z. It is important to note that bolt connectors transmit moment and torsion loads. Most hand calculations assume that bolts (and rivets) only transmit an axial and shear loads and ignore the moments and torsions. von Mises results will account for all directions.

33. Now try to display complete model results using ground plane and reflection settings.

34. Close File.

DP5 – Shell Analysis – Seed Hopper

(Design Problem Courtesy of Simba Great Plains Ltd)

Key features and workflows introduced in this design problem

	Key Features/Workflows
1	Edge Fixed Constraint
2	Surface Model – Connected Surfaces No Gaps
3	Advanced Mesh Settings
4	Global and Local Edge Mesh Control
5	Manual Shell Idealization
6	Continuous Mesh Connections
7	Shell Results Processing
8	Redesign

Introduction

On 30th April 2010, Simba International Limited was acquired by Great Plains Mfg., Inc, based in Salina, Kansas, USA bringing together the product innovation, expertise, experience and knowledge of two of the world's leading brands in tillage equipment. Simba Great Plains mainly cater for the agricultural industry and a typical product is a seed hopper as illustrated below.

In this design problem we are going to analyse the hopper using a simplified surface model using the following design information and goal.

Design Information

Material - **Stainless Steel AIS1 309**
Youngs Modulus - **200GPa**
Yield Limit - **344.7MPa**
Total Load - **30,000N**
Minimum F.O.S - **1.5**

Design Goal
Stress meets minimum F.O.S criteria.

Other Info
Maximum thickness of material to be used for main hopper body not to exceed 3mm.

Workflow of Design Problem 5

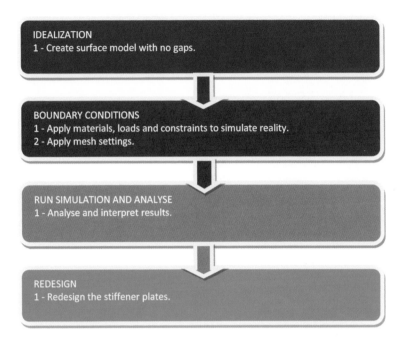

IDEALIZATION
1 - Create surface model with no gaps.

BOUNDARY CONDITIONS
1 - Apply materials, loads and constraints to simulate reality.
2 - Apply mesh settings.

RUN SIMULATION AND ANALYSE
1 - Analyse and interpret results.

REDESIGN
1 - Redesign the stiffener plates.

Idealization

The hopper within this design problem is constructed from sheet metal parts and plates. This will result in a lot of gaps, which will normally get filled with welds during manufacture. These if left within the model can result in artificially high stress values which will normally not exist in design.

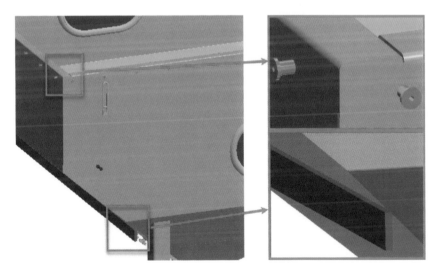

Alternatively, you can simplify the model as a connected surface like in this design problem.

CHAPTER 6

DP5 – Shell Analysis – Seed Hopper

All the non-structural items have been removed from the surface models including fasteners, seed dividers and other accessories as shown below.

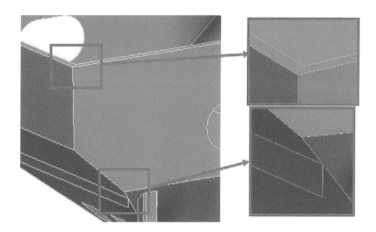

1.   Open *Hopper-surface.ipt*

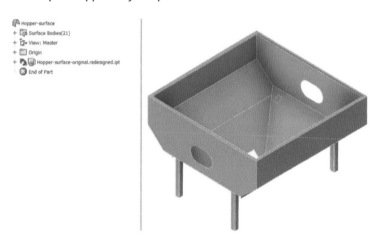

2.   Select and apply **Stainless Steel AISI 309** material from the Autodesk Material library.

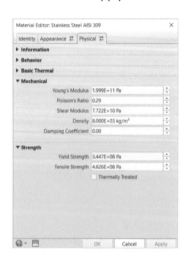

Boundary conditions

3.   Select **Environments** tab > Select **Autodesk Inventor Nastran**.

4.   Select **Idealizations** tab > Select **Shell Elements** for Type of Idealizations > Specify **Main Body** for Name of Idealization > > Select **Associative Geometry** > Select all the surfaces of the main hopper body > Specify **3mm** for t.

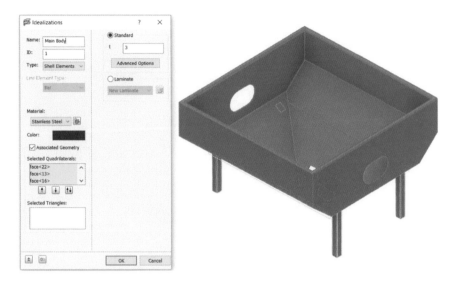

💡 Quicker to select multiple surfaces using window selection.

5.   Click **OK** > Select **Idealizations** tab again > Select **Shell Elements** for Type of Idealizations > Specify **Support Plates** for Name of Idealization > Select **Associative Geometry** > Select both surfaces underneath the main hopper body > Specify **10mm** for t.

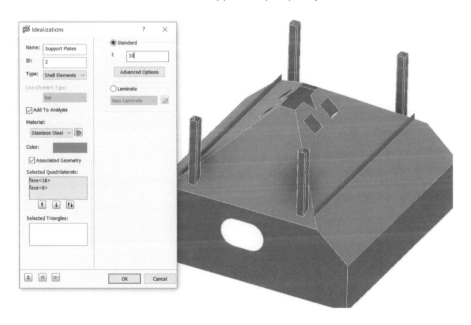

6.   Click **OK** > Select **Idealizations** tab again > Select **Shell Elements** for Type of Idealizations > Specify **Legs** for Name of Idealization > Select **Associative Geometry** > Select all four surfaces representing legs of hopper > Specify **8mm** for t.

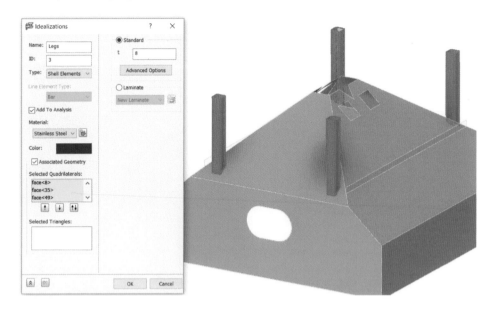

💡 Quicker to select multiple surfaces using crossing window selection or alternatively you can use face chain option from the Selected Quadrilaterals selection box by right clicking.

7.   Click **OK** > Select **Constraints** > Specify **Fixed Constraints** for Name > Select all bottom edges of all leg surfaces to apply constraint > Select **Preview** so you can adjust display options as desired.

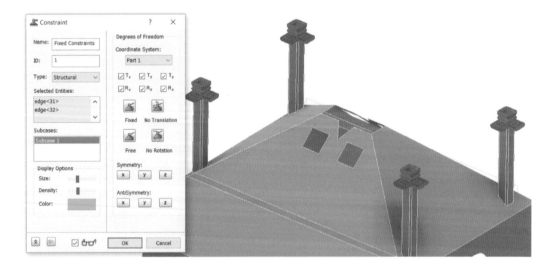

8. Click **OK** > Select **Loads** > Specify **Seed Load** for Name > Select **Components** for Direction, if not already selected > Specify **-30000** for Magnitude in Fy field > Select all internal surfaces at an angle as shown below > Select **Total Force** > **Select Preview** so you can adjust display options as desired.

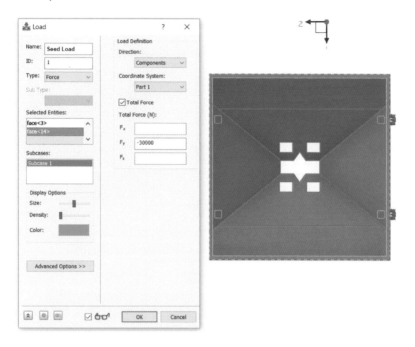

9. Click **OK** > Select **Mesh Settings** > Specify **25** for Element Size (mm) > Select **Continuous Meshing** > Select **Settings** to access Advanced Mesh Settings > Specify **1.1** for Max Element Growth Rate > Select **Project Midside Nodes** > Click **OK** > Select **Generate Mesh**.

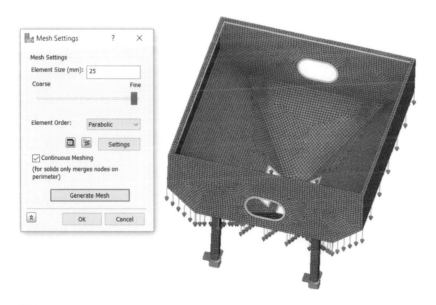

The bold white edge lines indicate free edges. This can be helpful in pinpointing surfaces at connections which are not connected.

As the surfaces are connected at the nodes as shown below there is no need to create contacts.

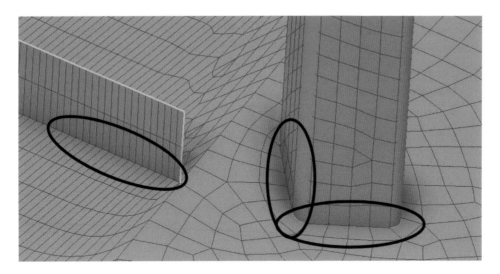

10. Click **OK** > Select **Mesh Control** > Select Edge Data option by clicking in the Selected Edges box > Select **Element Size** option > Specify **5** for Element Size (mm) > Select all the edges connecting the main hopper body and all four legs.

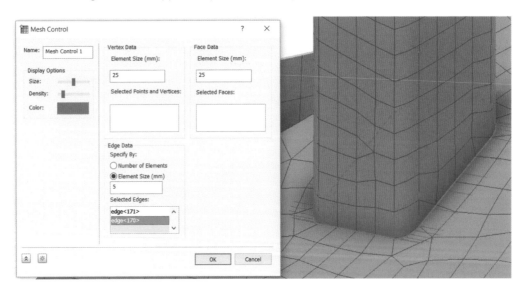

11. Click **OK** > Select **Generate Mesh** > Select **Object Visibility** > Unselect **Mesh Controls**.

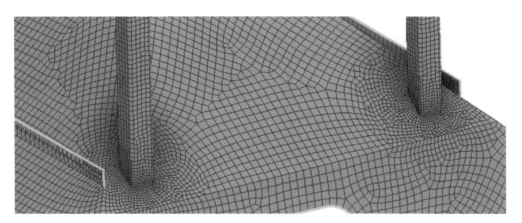

Run simulation and analyse

12. Select **Run** > Click **OK** when run is complete.

13. Right Click **von Mises stress** plot >Select **Edit** > Select **Specify Min/Max** value > Specify **0** for Data Min value > Specify **344** for Data Max value > Select **Visibility Options** > Hide **Loads** > Hide **Constraints** > Hide **Element Edges** > Select **Display**.

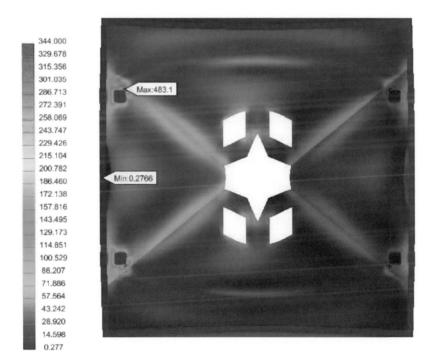

The maximum stress (nodal average based) is 483.1MPa which is above the material yield value. This suggest the material may locally yield around the leg and hopper body connection area. More importantly the design fails under the design goal requirement of minimum F.O.S being below 1.5.

DP5 – Shell Analysis – Seed Hopper

Suggesting the maximum stress value should not exceed 229.8MPa. This needs further investigating to see how we can reduce the stress value.

14. Click **OK** > Right click **Displacement** plot > Select **Edit** > Select **Section View** > Modify plane position so it cuts through the model after the max displacement position as shown below.

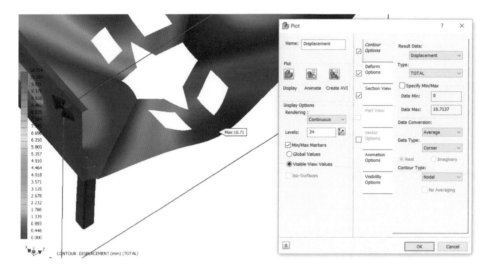

Maximum displacement is 10.71mm.

15. Click **OK** > Select **Animate**.

From further investigation we can see that legs are deflecting inwards along the Z-axis direction as shown below.

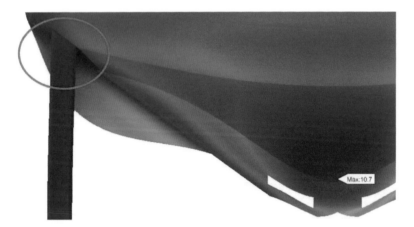

There is no deflection of the legs along the X-axis direction

16. Unselect **Animate**.

By reducing the leg deflections along Z-axis direction will help to reduce stress around the current high stress area.

Redesign – The stiffener plates

In this design problem we cannot increase the thickness of the hopper body as we are already using the maximum thickness of 3mm. So, we need to consider adding stiffening plates underneath the hopper body to reduce deflection and stress.

Below is one possible redesign solution or you could come up with your own alternative redesign.

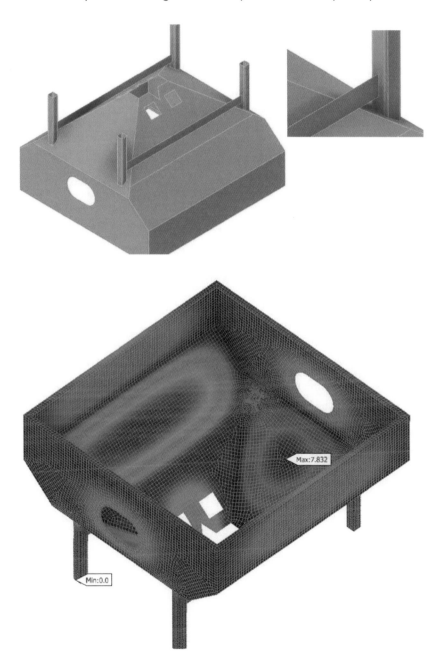

Maximum displacement reduced to 7.832mm

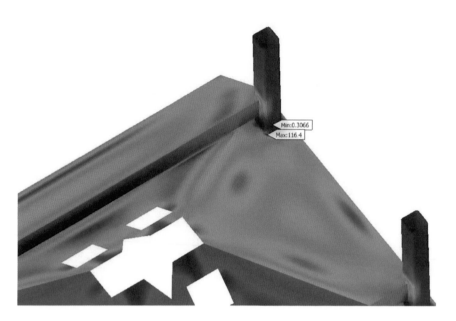

Maximum Stress is 116.4MPa (based on centroidal average)

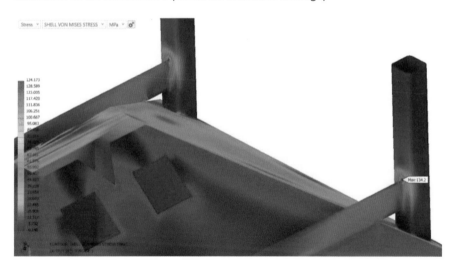

Maximum Stress is 134.2MPa (based on nodal average).

In both cases the stresses are below the design limit of 229.8MPa.

17. Close File.

DP6 – Shell Analysis – Base frame

(Design Problem Courtesy of Howden Compressors)

Key features and workflows introduced in this design problem

	Key Features/Workflows
1	**Gravity Load**
2	**Rigid Body Connectors**
3	**Idealizations - Concentrated Masses**
4	**Automatic Shell Idealizations**
5	**Mixed Solid and Shell Element Modelling**
6	**Automatic Solver Contacts**
7	**Part Mesh Control**
8	**Shell and Solid Results**

CHAPTER 7
DP6 – Shell Analysis – Base frame

Introduction

Howdens are a global engineering business who focus on providing their clients with industrial products that help multiple sectors improve their everyday processes; from mine ventilation and waste water treatment to heating and cooling. Howden Compressors with more than a century of applications experience and a range that covers every major technology can advise on design and supply the right compressor for virtually any situation. Below is a typical unit.

In this design problem we are going to analyse the base frame using automatic mid surface idealizations using the following design information and goal.

Design Information

Main Structure
Material - **BS EN 10025 S275JR**
Youngs Modulus - **210GPa**
Yield Limit - **207MPa**
Load - **Weight of primary components**
Minimum F.O.S - **1.5**

Lifting Eye
Material - **BS EN 10025 S355JR**
Youngs Modulus - **200GPa**
Yield Limit - **350MPa**
Load - **Weight of primary components**
Minimum F.O.S - **1.5**

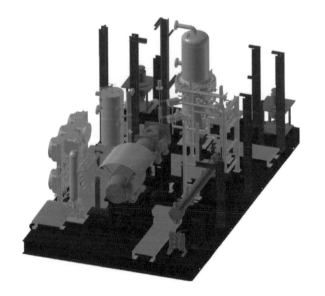

Design Goal
Stress meets minimum F.O.S criteria.

Workflow of Design Problem 6

IDEALIZATION
1 - Idealize thin parts with mid-surfaces, automatically.
2 - Idealize assembly component masses with a single concentrated mass.

BOUNDARY CONDITIONS
1 - Apply materials, loads and constraints to simulate reality.
2 - Apply mesh settings.

RUN SIMULATION AND ANALYSE
1 - Analyse and interpret results.

REDESIGN
1 - None.

Idealization

The complete Howden unit comprises of many components including a compressor, motor, primary separator, auxiliary unit's pipework and other support systems as illustrated below.

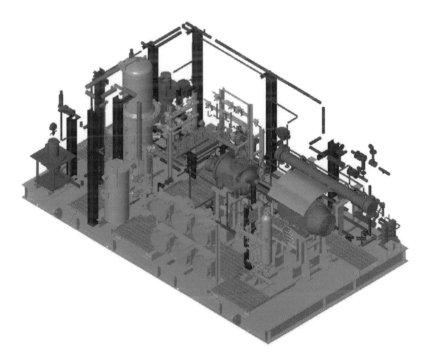

The complete unit contains far too much information for the purposes of this design problem plus the need to reduce the file size considerably.

CHAPTER 7

DP6 – Shell Analysis – Base frame

The illustration below shows the model significantly simplified by accounting for some of the main components including the primary and secondary separator units.

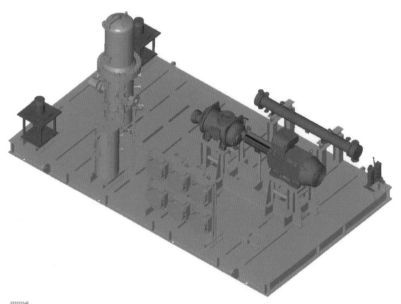

In practice all components will be accounted for to get accurate results.

In this design problem as we are only interested in accounting for the weights of the main components on the base frame. We can further simplify the main components into single concentrated masses, within Inventor Nastran as illustrated below.

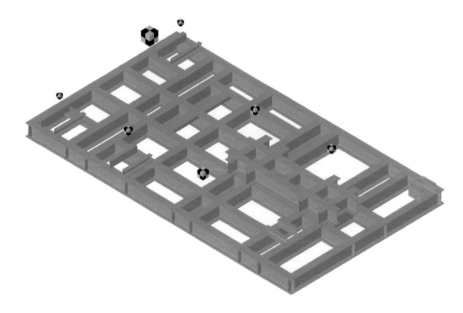

1. Open *Separator – Unit.iam*

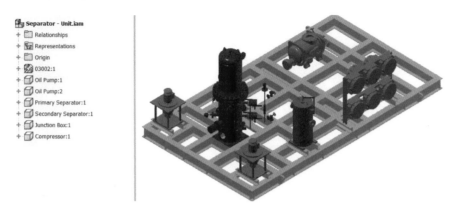

Boundary conditions

2. Select **Environments** tab > Select **Autodesk Inventor Nastran**.

This will automatically create 24 beam elements as the base structures where created using frame generator.

3. Right click **Beams** Idealization under the Model tree > Select **Delete All**.

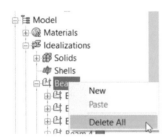

This will permanently delete the idealizations from the file including removing them from the analysis.

4. If the main components (excluding frame) are invisible, then follow the next step otherwise go straight to step 6.

5. Right click components as shown below > Select **Visibility**.

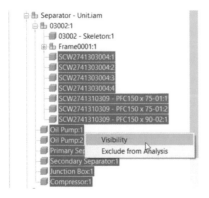

CHAPTER 7

DP6 – Shell Analysis – Base frame

6. Select **Solid2** and **Solid3** Idealizations under the Model tree > Right click selection > Select **Delete** > Click **OK**.

7. Select **Generic** materials > Right click selection > Select **Delete**.

In the following steps we are going to idealise the key components into concentrated masses automatically so that we can take their weight into consideration when analysing the base frame.

Components	Mass (tonne/mm³)
Primary Separator	7.753e-9
Secondary Separator	6.189e-9
Compressor	7.870e-9
Junction Box	7.860e-9
Oil Pumps	4.770e-9

Inventor Nastran only requires the density value of the components to calculate the masses. Plus, the default mass units in Inventor Nastran are in tonne/mm³.

8. Select **Concentrated Masses** under Idealizations in the model tree > Right click > Select **New**.

9. Specify **Compressor** for Name > Select **Automatic** > Select **Motor** > Specify **7.87e-9** for Density.

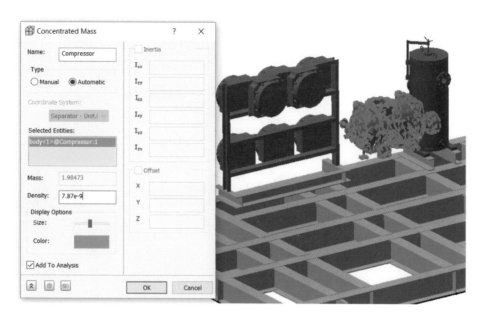

10. Click **OK**.

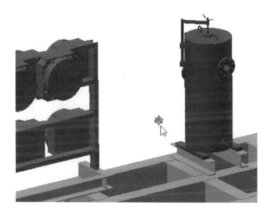

Concentrated mass is currently only capable of selecting single components. So, you will need to either derive assembly into a single part, like here, or shrink-wrap assembly substitute as a level of detail.

11. Repeat step 8-10 for the remaining components.

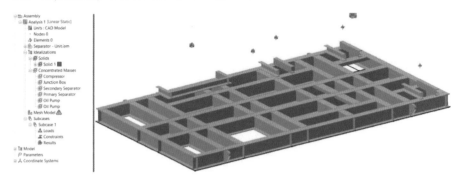

12. Select **Midsurface** > Select all members using window selection moving from left to right, making sure you do not cover the lifting eyes completely by the window selection.

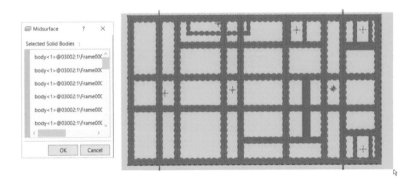

Alternatively, you can use Find Thin Bodies to automatically select components.

13. Click **OK**.

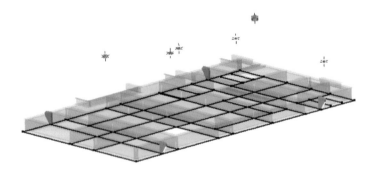

Now we are going to connect the lumped masses to the base frame.

14. Select **Connector** > Select **Rigid Body** for type > Activate **Select Point** by clicking in the selection box > Select **Oil Pump** Concentrated Mass sketch point.

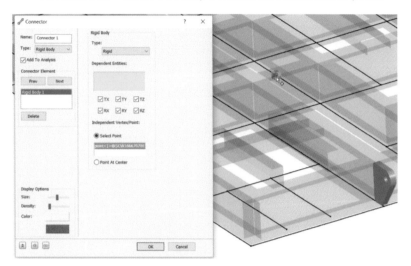

15. Select the two highlighted faces as shown for Dependent Entities.

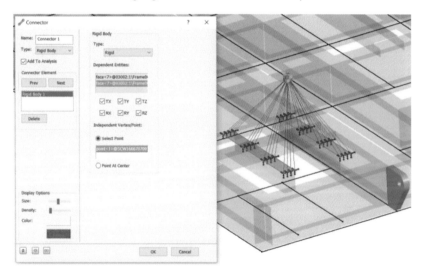

16. Select **Next** for Connector Element.

17. Activate **Select Point** by clicking in the selection box > Select **Oil Pump** Concentrated Mass 2 sketch point.

18. Select the two faces as shown for Dependent Entities.

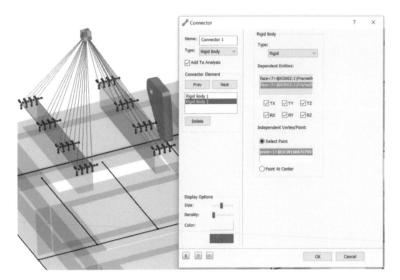

19. Select **Next** for Connector Element.

20. Activate **Select Point** by clicking in the selection box > Select **Primary Separator** Concentrated Mass sketch point.

21. Select the two highlighted faces as shown for Dependent Entities.

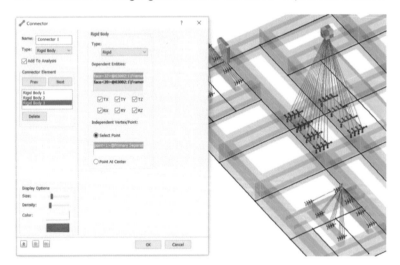

The structures have been split to spread the load on a certain area of the structure.

22. Select **Next** for Connector Element.

23. Activate **Select Point** by clicking in the selection box > Select **Secondary Separator** Concentrated Mass sketch point.

24. Select the two highlighted faces as shown for Dependent Entities.

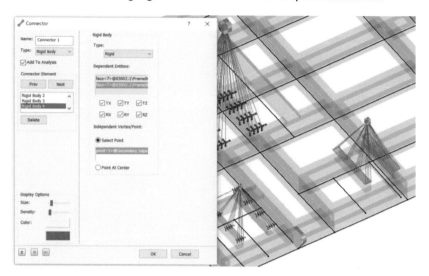

25. Select **Next** for Connector Element.

26. Activate **Select Point** by clicking in the selection box > Select **Junction Box** Concentrated Mass sketch point.

27. Select the three faces as shown for Dependent Entities.

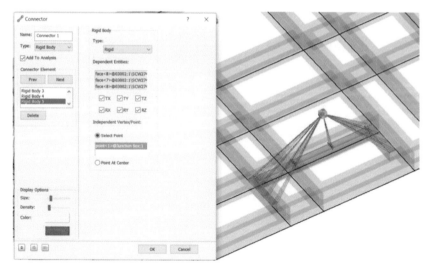

28. Select **Next** for Connector Element.

29. Activate **Select Point** by clicking in the selection box > Select **Compressor** Concentrated Mass sketch point.

30. Select the two faces as shown for Dependent Entities.

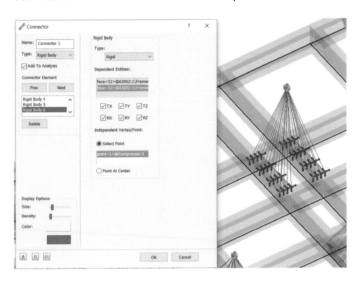

31. Click **OK**.

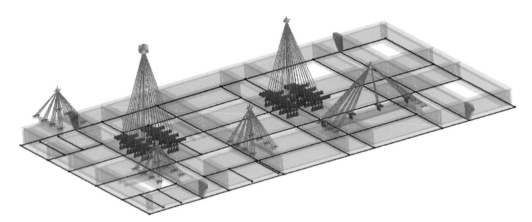

32. Select **Pin Constraints** > Select **Fix Radial Direction** > Fix **Axial Direction** > Select internal face of the hole as shown.

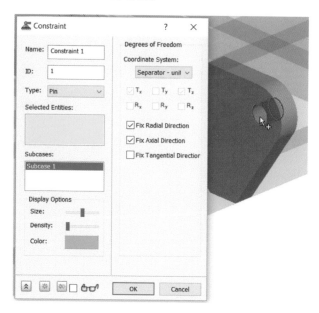

33. Click **OK**.

34. Repeat **32** for the remaining three lifting eyes.

35. Select **Loads** > Specify **Gravity** for Name > Select **Gravity** for load type > Specify **-9810** for Magnitude in Fz field > Click **OK**.

36. Select **Mesh Settings** > Specify **50** for Element Size (mm) > Select **Settings** to access Advanced Mesh Settings > Select **Project Midside Nodes** > Click **OK** twice.

37. Select **Mesh Control** > Select Part Data option by clicking in the Selected Parts box > Select **Element Size** option > Specify **25** for Element Size (mm) > Select all the lifting eye parts.

38. Click **OK** > Select **Generate Mesh**.

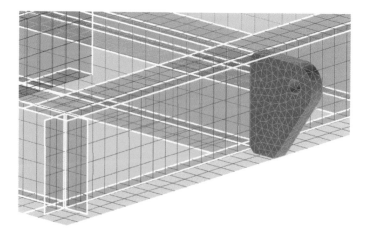

39. Select **Solver** Contact > Specify **Offset Bonded** for contact type > Specify **20** for max activation distance (mm).

 Always use a Solver Contact when the model contains surfaces with gaps.

 You always need to specify a Max Activation Distance (mm) value when using Midsurfaces button. Specify a value which covers the biggest gap between the surfaces.

40. Click **OK**.

Run simulation and analyse

41. Select **Run** > Click **OK** once run is complete.

42. Select **Object Visibility** > Unselect **Connectors** > Unselect **Constraints** > Unselect **Concentrated Masses** > Unselect **Deformed** from the Results panel.

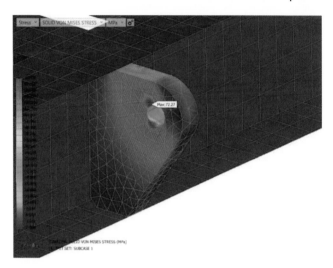

The maximum solid von Mises stress in the lifting eyes is 72.27MPa. This stress is a lot higher in reality as this exercise has only included partial load.

> If CAD bodies become visible. You will need to unselect visibility by right clicking the solids in the browser tree.

43. Select **Shell Max Principal Mises Stress Bottom/Top** from the results bar within the graphic window.

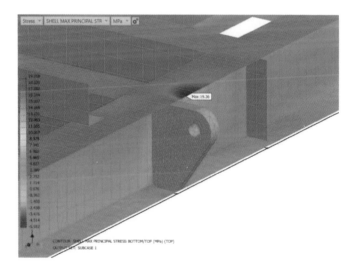

The maximum Shell von Mises stress is 19.358MPa.

> In the current version of Inventor Nastran, you cannot look at solid and shell results together.

44. Select **Displacement** results

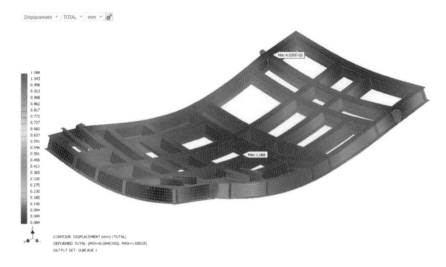

The maximum displacement is 1mm.

45. Close File.

DP7 – Beam Analysis – Platform

(Design Problem Courtesy of Planet Platforms Ltd)

Key features and workflows introduced in this design problem

	Key Features/Workflows
1	**Point Fixed Constraints**
2	**Edge Force Load**
3	**Manual Line Idealizations**
4	**Cross Section Properties**
5	**Cross Section Display**
6	**Bar Orientations**
7	**Bar Results**
8	**Redesign**

Introduction

Planet Platforms is a leading manufacturer and distributor of work place access solutions. Through a process of communication, site surveys, CAD and proven manufacturing, Planet Platform delivers the end result – a platform that is safe, reliable and perfectly suited for the application. Below is a typical example of a maintenance platform.

In this design problem we are going to analyse the maintenance platform with bar elements using the following design information and goal.

Design Information

Material - **Aluminium**
Youngs Modulus - **68.9GPa**
Yield Limit - **275MPa**
Load - **2500N**
Minimum F.O.S - **2**

Design Goal
Stress meets minimum F.O.S criteria.

Workflow of Design Problem 7

IDEALIZATION
1 - Remove non-structural items.
2 - Represent structures with line elements.

BOUNDARY CONDITIONS
1 - Apply materials, loads and constraints to simulate reality.
2 - Apply mesh settings.

RUN SIMULATION AND ANALYSE
1 - Analyse and interpret results.

REDESIGN
1 - Reduce size of cross sections.

Idealization

In this example all the non-structural items like hand-rails, wheels, fasteners, step and platform mesh will not be included in the analysis, as shown below.

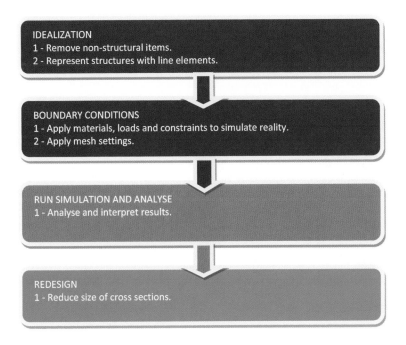
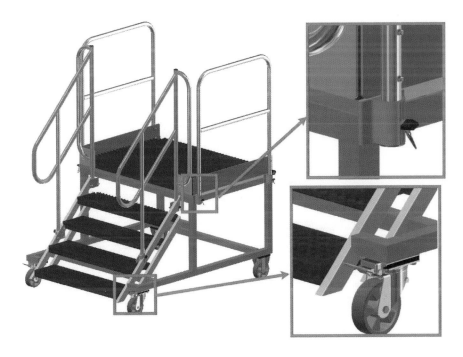

CHAPTER 8

DP7 – Beam Analysis – Platform

As Inventor Nastran allows to populate 3D wireframe models with 3D cross sectional properties the structural assembly of the platform will be further simplified to a 3D sketch model as shown below.

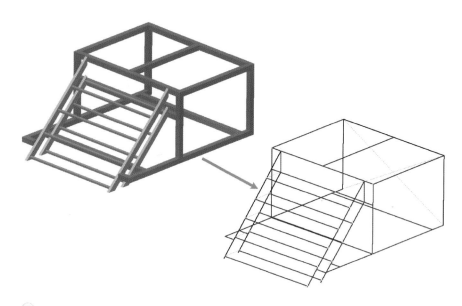

Populating a 3D sketch model will generate far less beam idealizations than the automatic beam idealizations.

1.   Open *Main-structure.ipt*

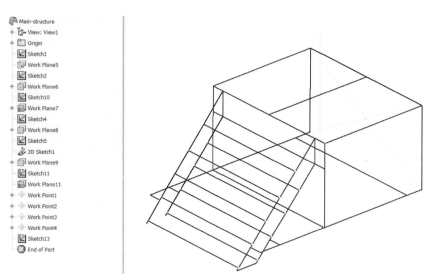

Boundary conditions

2. Select **Environments** tab > Select **Autodesk Inventor Nastran**.

No idealization will be automatically defined as the model only contains lines and points.

3. Select **Idealizations** > Select **Line Elements** for element type > Specify **50x50x3** for Name > Select **Cross Section** for input type > Select **New material** icon > Select **Aluminium** from Inventor Material library > Click **OK** twice > Select **Associated Geometry** > Select all lines except the steps.

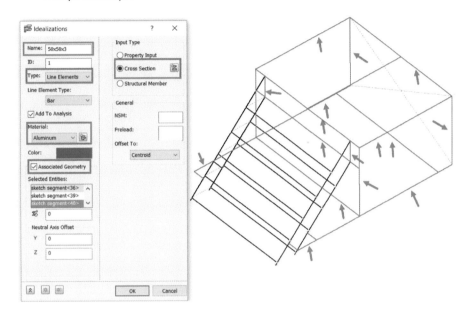

4. Click on **Cross Section Definition** icon > Select **Box** for shape definition > Specify **50** for DIM1 > Specify **50** DIM2 > Specify **3** for DIM3 > Specify **3** for DIM4 > Select **Draw End A** to populate cross sectional properties.

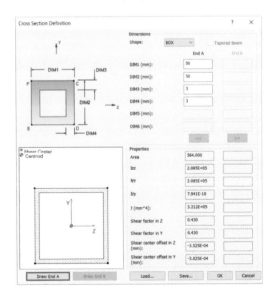

5. Click **OK** twice > Select **Idealizations** again > Select **Line Elements** for element type > Specify **25x25x3** for Name > Select **Cross Section** for input type > Select **Aluminium** from material list > Select **Associated Geometry** > Select all lines on the steps, except the one indicated by the arrow below (top step structure).

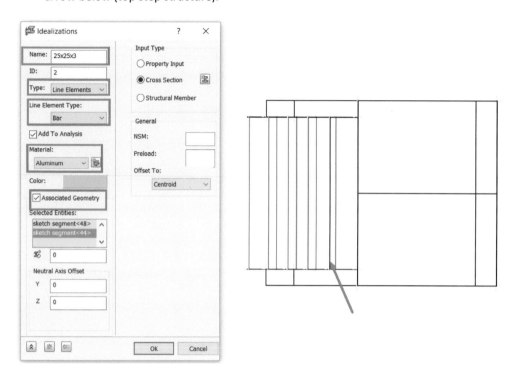

6. Click on **Cross Section Definition** icon > Select **Box** for shape definition > Specify **25** for DIM1 > Specify **25** DIM2 > Specify **3** for DIM3 > Specify **3** for DIM4 > Select **Draw End A** to populate cross sectional properties.

7. Click **OK** twice > Select **Idealizations** again > Select **Line Elements** for element type > Specify **Top Step** for Name > Select **Cross Section** for input type > Select **Aluminium** from material list > Select **Associated Geometry** > Select the line indicated by arrow below.

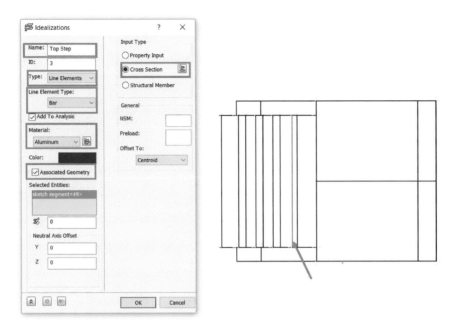

8. Click on **Cross Section Definition** icon > Select **Box** for shape definition > Specify **25** for DIM1 > Specify **25** DIM2 > Specify **3** for DIM3 > Specify **3** for DIM4 > Select **Draw End A** to populate cross sectional properties.

9. Click **OK** twice > Select **Idealizations** again > Specify **80x20x3** for Name > Select **Line Elements** for element type > Select **Cross Section** for input type > Select **Aluminium** from material list > Select **Associated Geometry** > Select all the diagonal lines on the steps as shown below.

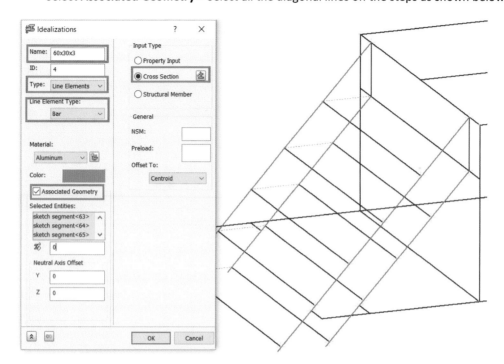

10. Click on **Cross Section Definition** icon > Select **Box** for shape definition > Specify **20** for DIM1 > Specify **80** DIM2 > Specify **3** for DIM3 > Specify **3** for DIM4 > Select **Draw End A** to populate cross sectional properties > Click **OK** twice.

11. Select **Mesh Settings** > Specify **20** for Element Size (mm) > Select **Continuous Meshing** > Click **OK**.

12. Right click **Elements** > Select **Display Cross Section**.

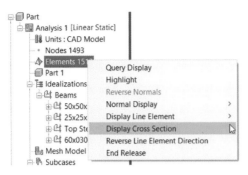

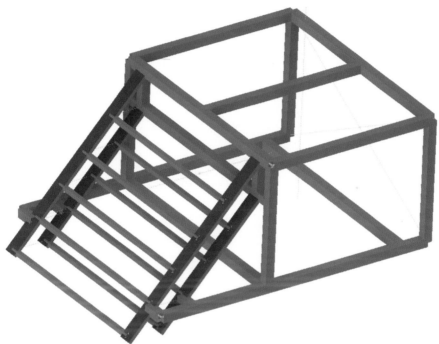

The orientation of the 80x20x3 idealization needs rotating by 90 degrees plus need to offset the top step idealization by 12.5mm so it's in line with the main structure as shown below.

This is why we created a separate idealization for the top step so we can modify beam idealization for top step only.

13. Double click **80x20x3** beam idealization > Specify **90** for rotation angle.

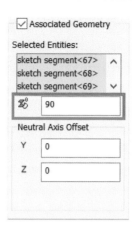

14. Click **OK** > Double click **Top Step beam** idealization > Specify **12.5** for Y Neutral Axis Offset.

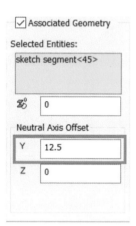

15. Click **OK**.

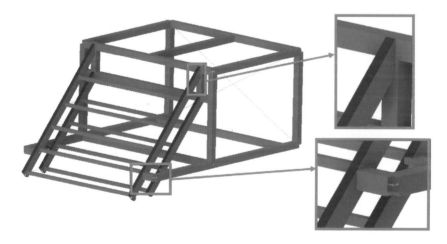

16. Right click **Elements** > Unselect **Display Cross Section** > Select **Constraints** > Specify **Fixed Constraints** for Name > Select the ends of the four beams as shown below.

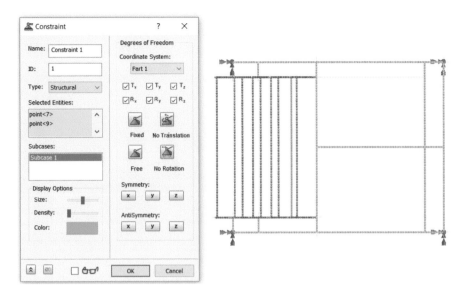

17. Click **OK.**

18. Select **Loads** > Specify **Total Load** for Name > Select **Components** for Direction, if not already selected > Specify **-2500** for Magnitude in Fy field > Select all the lines directly under the platform deck as shown > Select **Total Force** > **Select Preview** so you can adjust display options as desired.

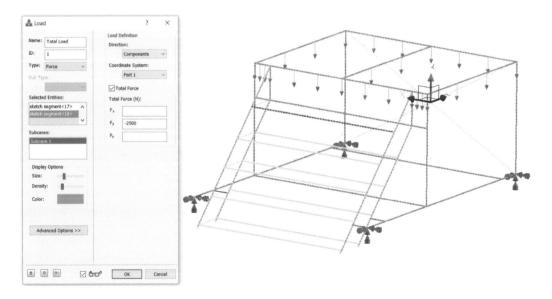

19. Click **OK**.

Run simulation and analyse

20.   Select **Run** > Click **OK** once run is complete.

21.   Select **Bar von Mises stress** plot, if not already selected > Deselect **Deformed** results.

22.   Select **Object Visibility** > Unselect **Constraints** > Unselect **Loads**.

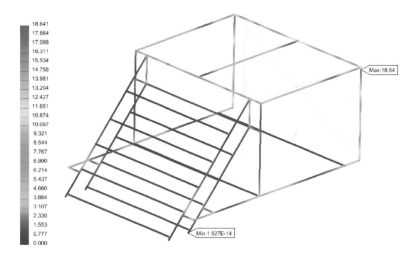

The maximum stress is 18.64MPa.

23.   Select **Displacement** plot.

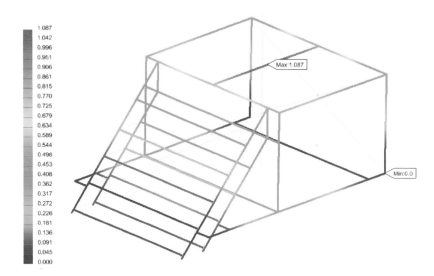

The maximum displacement is 1.087mm.

This design is overdesigned. The factor of safety for this design is 14.75.

$$Factor\ of\ Safety = \frac{275}{18.64} = 14.75$$

So, we need to optimize the design.

Redesign – Reduce size of cross sections

Below is a sample redesign and results for your consideration.

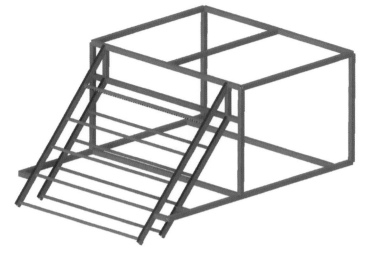

Main Structure
Box Section 30x30x2

Steps
Box Section 15x15x2
Box Section 40x20x2

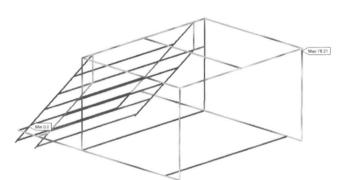

Maximum Stress is 78.21MPa

$$Factor\ of\ Safety = \frac{275}{78.21} = 3.5$$

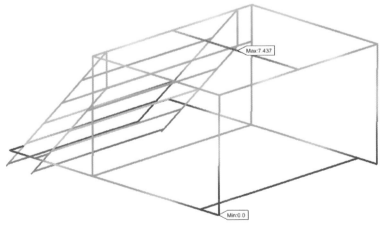

Maximum Displacement
is 7.437mm

24. Close File.

DP8 – Beam Analysis – Gangway

(Design Problem courtesy of Tyne Gangway (Structures) Ltd)

Key features and workflows introduced in this design problem

	Key Features/Workflows
1	**Edge Rolling Constraints**
2	**Edge Distributed Load**
3	**Automatic Line Idealizations**
4	**Bar results – including forces**
5	**Reaction Forces**

CHAPTER 9
DP8 – Beam Analysis – Gangway

Introduction

Established in 1934 Tyne Gangway (Structures) limited has gained an enviable reputation as a successful company with excellent gangway design and manufacturing techniques coupled with superb customer service. The company specialises in the design and manufacture of aluminium gangways, accommodation ladders, shore based pedestrian access equipment, special structures, and has a Worldwide oil, gas, shipping and marine customer base.

In this design problem we are going to analyse the gangway using automatic line idealizations using the following design information and goal.

Design Information

Main Structure
Material - **Aluminium**
Youngs Modulus - **71GPa**
Yield Limit - **280MPa**
Load - **5000N/m²**
Minimum F.O.S - **1.5**

Design Goal
Stress meets minimum F.O.S criteria.

Workflow of Design Problem 8

IDEALIZATION
1 - Remove non-structural items.

BOUNDARY CONDITIONS
1 - Apply materials, loads and constraints to simulate reality.
2 - Apply mesh settings.

RUN SIMULATION AND ANALYSE
1 - Analyse and interpret results.

OPTIMIZATION
1 - None.

Idealization

The gangway used in this example, as illustrated below, includes ramps, wheels, fixture and fittings step threads and more.

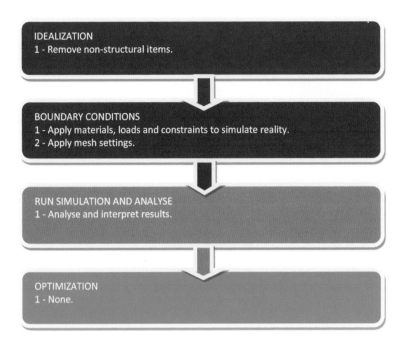

CHAPTER 9

DP8 – Beam Analysis – Gangway

For analysis purposes the gangway is stripped down to include only the main structure of the gangway as illustrated below.

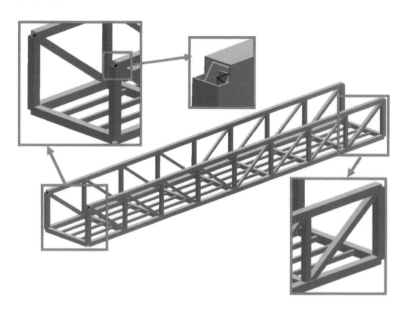

The current version of Inventor Nastran automatically creates beam idealizations if the structures have been created using frame generator. Content centre structures are not currently supported.

1.   Open *Gangway.iam*

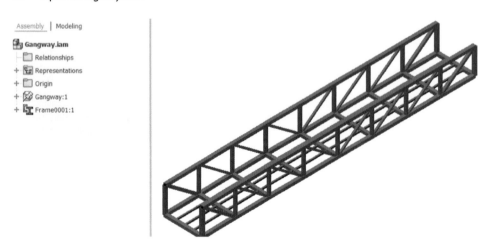

Boundary conditions

2.   Select **Environments** tab > Select **Autodesk Inventor Nastran**.

50 Beam Idealization will be automatically created as the structures was built using frame generator.

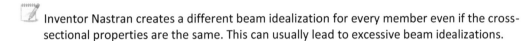

Inventor Nastran creates a different beam idealization for every member even if the cross-sectional properties are the same. This can usually lead to excessive beam idealizations.

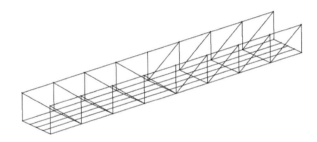

3.   Select **Constraints** > Specify **Fixed Constraints** for Name > Select the corner of the edges as shown > Select **Preview** so you can adjust display options as desired.

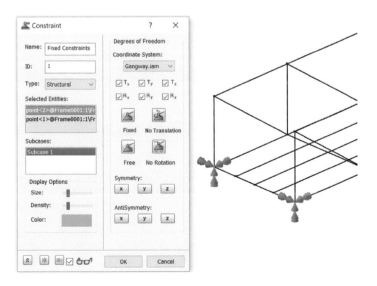

4.   Click **OK** > Press **spacebar** to apply constraints again.

5.   Specify **Rolling Constraints** for Name > Select the edge at the other end as shown > Select **Y Symmetry** > Select **Preview** so you adjust display options as desired.

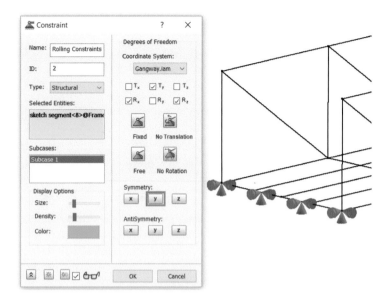

This constraint will simulate a roller type constraint which is free to move in horizontal plane.

6.   Click **OK**

Next, we need to apply the following 5KN/m^2 load on the gangway structure.

First, we need to convert the load to Newtons by working out the free area of the gangway.

Load = Length X free width X Load/m^2

Load = 12 x 1.375 x 5 = 82.5KN.

Next, we distribute this load equally across the members placed along the full length of the gangway (9 in total).

Load per cross member = 82.5KN/9 = 9.17KN

Finally, to work the distributed load per member we divide the load by the length of the member.

Distributed Load = 9.17KN/1525mm = 6N/mm

7.   Select **Loads** > Specify **Total Load** for Name > Select **Distributed Load** from Load Type > Select **Components** for Direction, if not already selected > Specify **-6** for Magnitude in Fy field > Select all horizontal cross members as shown below > **Select Preview** so you can adjust display options as desired.

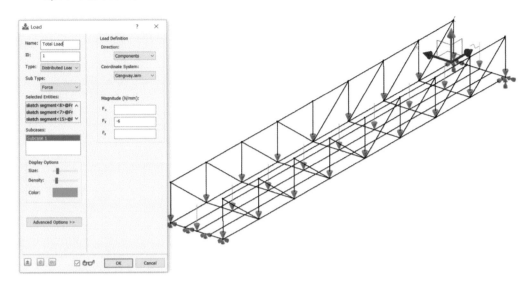

8.   Click **OK** > Select **Mesh Settings** > Specify **100** for Element Size (mm) > Select **Generate Mesh**.

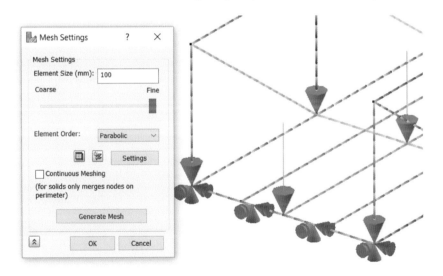

9. Click **OK** > Right click **Analysis 1** > Select **Edit** > Select **Force** from Elemental Output Sets.

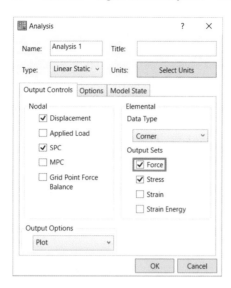

This will allow us to view force results

10. Click **OK**.

Run simulation and analyse

11. Select **Run** > Click **OK** when run is complete.

12. Select **Displacement** plot.

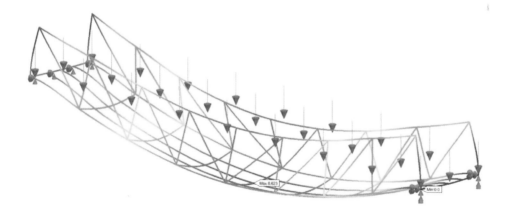

The maximum displacement is 8.623mm in the middle of the gangway.

13. Select **Animate**.

We can see there is horizontal movement at the rolling constraint end.

14. Deselect **Animate** > Select **von Mises** plot > Select **Deformed** > Select **Object Visibility** > Deselect **Loads** > Deselect **Constraints**.

We can see the maximum stress value of 26.73MPa is at the fixed end position. This is well below our design safety factor.

15. Right Click **Fixed Constraints** > Select **SPC Summation**.

16. Click **Close** > Right Click **Rolling Constraints** > Select **SPC Summation**.

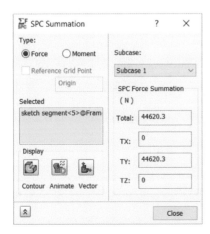

The excess load of 6708N (44587.7 + 44620.3- 82500 = 6708) is due to the weight of the gangway approximately 680kg.

17. Right Click **Results** > Select **New** > Specify **Beam Forces** for Name > Select **Beam Diagram** for Result Data > Select **Bar Force End A-X** for Type of data > Unselect **Beam Diagrams** > Select **Maximum** for Data Conversion.

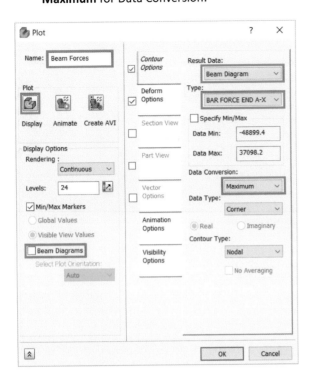

Selecting Maximum will allow us see results at nodes rather than seeing average results anywhere along the beam element.

18. Select **Display**.

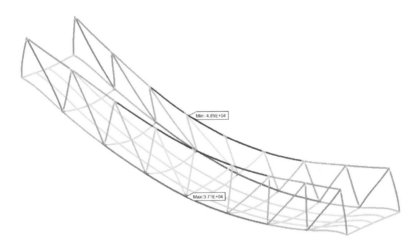

The maximum tensile axial force in the gangway is 37098N.

Below is some information of what the result types mean.

Type	Result
Bar Force End A-X	Axial Force
Bar Force End A-Y Plane 1	Shear Force in the local Y direction
Bar Force End A-Z Plane 2	Shear Force in the local Z direction
Bar Moment End A-X	Torsion in the bolt due to rotation.
Bar Moment End A-Y Plane 1	Moment about the local Y direction
Bar Moment End A-Z Plane 2	Moment about the local Z direction

Also End A and End B refer to the ends of the bar element.

Creating a new result creates another customized result plot as shown below

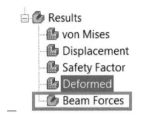

19. Click **OK**

20. Close File.

DP9 – Shell & Beam Analysis – Water Tank

Key features and workflows introduced in this design problem

	Key Features/Workflows
1	**Custom Coordinate Systems**
2	**Hydrostatic Load**
3	**Symmetry Conditions**
4	**Mixed Shell and Beam Element Modelling**
5	**Manual Shell Idealizations**
6	**Manual Line Idealization**
7	**Cross Section Properties**
8	**Continuous Meshing**
9	**Bar Results**
10	**Shell Results**
11	**Redesign**

Introduction

Water tanks are used to provide storage of water for use in many applications, drinking water, irrigation agriculture, fire suppression, agricultural farming, both for plants and livestock, chemical manufacturing, food preparation as well as many other uses. Below is a typical example of a standalone water tank made of plastic and aluminium support structure.

In this design problem we are going to analyse the water tank using shell and bar elements using the following design information and goal.

Design Information

Tank Body
Material - **ABS**
Youngs Modulus - **2.2GPa**
Yield Limit - **20MPa**
Minimum F.O.S - **2**
Thickness - **1.5mm**

Tank Body
Material - **Aluminium**
Youngs Modulus - **68.9GPa**
Yield Limit - **275MPa**
Minimum F.O.S - **4**
Box section - **30x30x3**
Box Section 2 - **10x10x1**

Design Goal
Stress meets minimum F.O.S criteria.

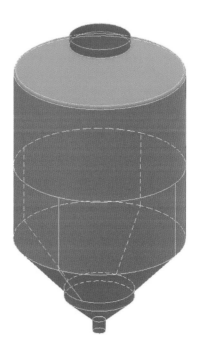

Workflow of Design Problem 9

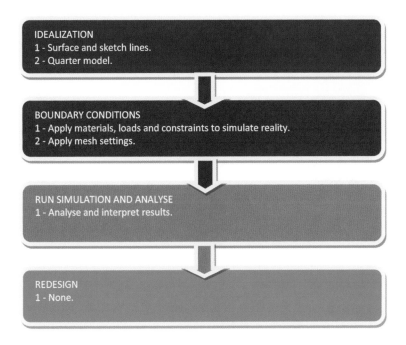

IDEALIZATION
1 - Surface and sketch lines.
2 - Quarter model.

BOUNDARY CONDITIONS
1 - Apply materials, loads and constraints to simulate reality.
2 - Apply mesh settings.

RUN SIMULATION AND ANALYSE
1 - Analyse and interpret results.

REDESIGN
1 - None.

Idealization

In this example the tank is simplified into a surface and sketch model. The surface model represents the tank and sketch models represents the structure to support the tank. Furthermore, the surfaces are split at locations where they are attached to a structure. This will aid in the connection of the shell and bar elements. Finally, the tank and supporting structure are further simplified into a quarter model.

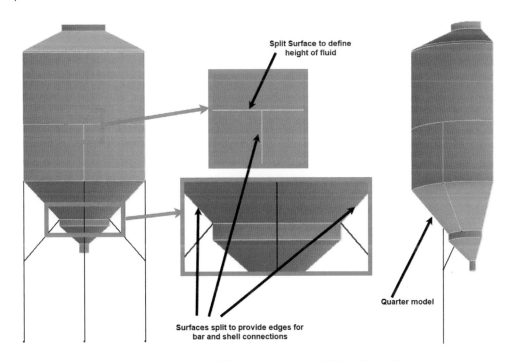

Split Surface to define height of fluid

Surfaces split to provide edges for bar and shell connections

Quarter model

CHAPTER 10

DP9 – Shell & Beam Analysis – Water Tank

1. Open *Water-tank.iam*

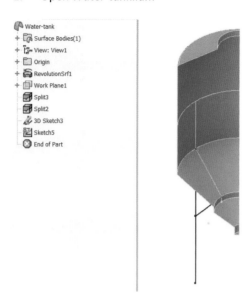

Boundary conditions

2. Select **Environments** tab > Select **Autodesk Inventor Nastran.**

No idealization will be automatically defined as the model only contains sketches and surfaces.

3. Select **Idealizations** > Select **Line Elements** for element type > Specify **30x30x3** for Name > Select **Cross Section** for input type > Select **New material** icon > Select **Aluminium** from Inventor Material library > Click **OK** twice > Select **Associated Geometry** > Select three vertical and four connecting curve edges as shown below.

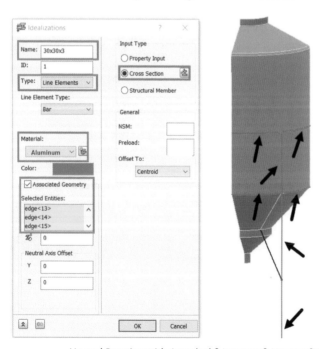

4. Click on **Cross Section Definition** icon > Select **Box** for shape definition > Specify **30** for DIM1 > Specify **30** DIM2 > Specify **3** for DIM3 > Specify **3** for DIM4 > Select **Draw End A** to populate cross sectional properties.

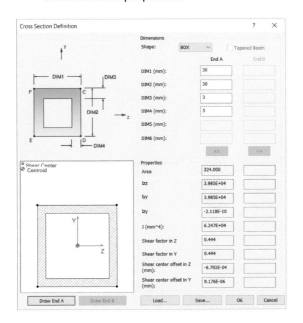

5. Click **OK** twice > Select **Idealizations** again > Select **Line Elements** for element type > Specify **10x10x1** for Name > Select **Cross Section** for input type > Select **Aluminium** from material list > Select **Associated Geometry** > Select all angled and connecting curve lines as shown below.

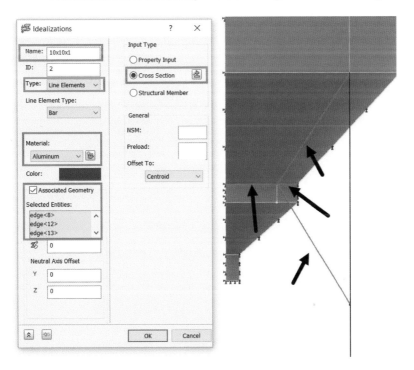

6.   Click on **Cross Section Definition** icon > Select **Box** for shape definition > Specify **10** for DIM1 > Specify **10** DIM2 > Specify **1** for DIM3 > Specify **1** for DIM4 > Select **Draw End A** to populate cross sectional properties.

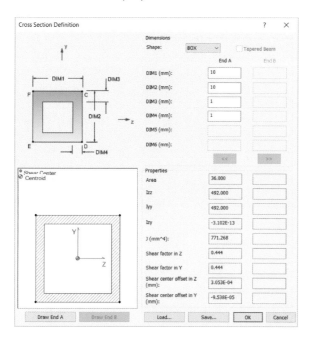

7.   Click **OK** twice.

8.   Select **Idealizations** again > Select **Shell Elements** for element type > Specify **Tank** for Name > Specify **1.5** for thickness > Select **ABS** from material list > Select **Associated Geometry** > Select faces using window selection around tank body to select all surfaces.

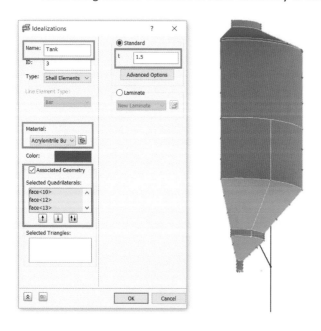

9. Click **OK** > Select **Constraints** > Specify **Fixed Constraints** for Name > Select the bottom end of the vertical edge as shown.

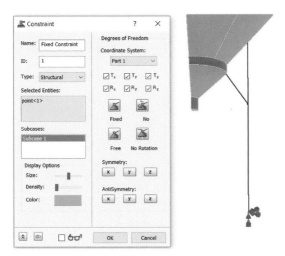

10. Click **OK**.

As we are modelling a quarter of a tank we need to define symmetry conditions. To do this we first need to specify a custom cylindrical coordinate system as none of the edges of the tank are in line with the global coordinate system and thus cannot use default x, y, z symmetry constraints.

11. Right click **Coordinate Systems** > Select **New**.

12. Select **Cylindrical** for Type > Specify **0,0,0** for Origin > Specify **0,1000,0** for Point on Z Axis > Select vertex on edge of tank as shown.

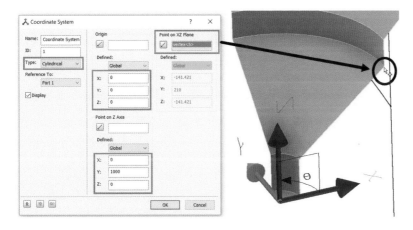

13. Click **OK**.

14. Select **Constraints** > Specify **Symmetry** for Name > Select **Coordinate System 1** for Coordinate System > Select **theta** for Symmetry > Select all edges on perimeter of the quarter tank except the top edge as highlighted by the arrow below.

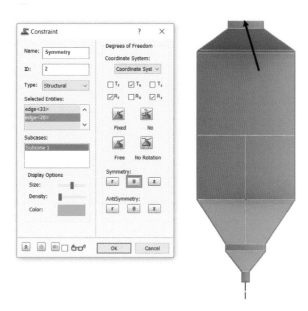

15. Click **OK** > Select **Object Visibility** > Unselect **Constraints**.

Next, we need to apply the load exerted by the fluid inside the tank (hydrostatic load).

16. Select **Loads** > Specify **Hydrostatic load** for Name > Select **Hydrostatic Load** from load type > Select all faces in contact with water as shown below (9 faces in total).

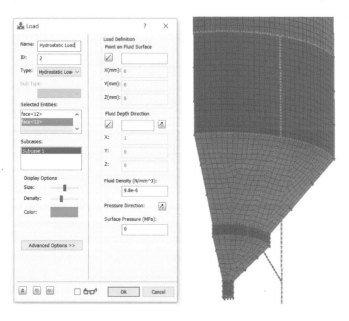

17. Select **Point on Fluid Surface** icon > Select point as shown below to define surface of water.

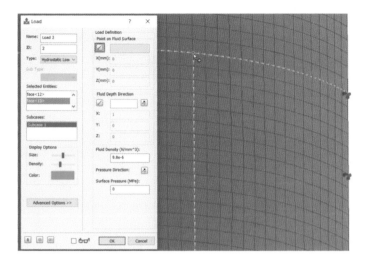

18. Select **Fluid Depth Direction** icon > Specify **0, -1, 0** for direction of fluid depth > Flip the direction of the pressure as shown below (pressure acting outwards). Density of water is already specified as the default value in N/mm^3.

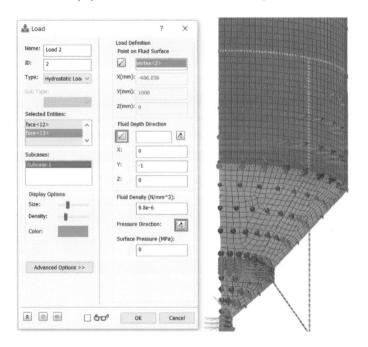

19. Click **OK** > Select **Mesh Settings** > Specify **25** for Element Size (mm) > Select **Continuous Meshing** > Select **Settings** to access Advanced Mesh Settings > Select **Project Midside Nodes** > Click **OK** twice.

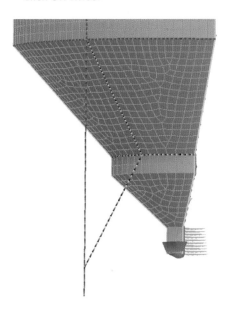

Run simulation and analyse

20. Select **Run** > Click **OK** when run is complete.

21. Select **Displacement** plot > Unselect **Deformed** > Select **Object Visibility** > Unselect **Loads**.

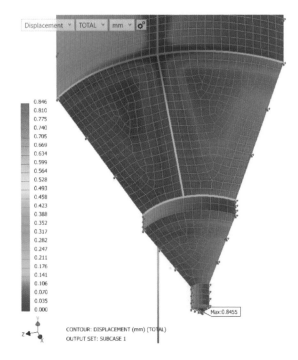

The maximum displacement is 0.846mm.

22. Select **Shell Max von Mises** stress plot.

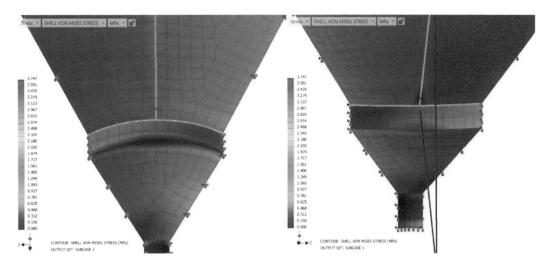

23. Select **Shell Max von Mises Bottom/Top** stress plot.

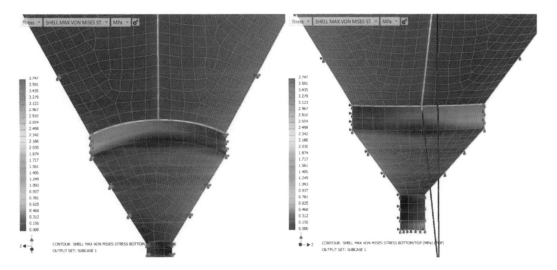

Shell Max von Mises Bottom/Top stress plots same max stress results on both sides of the shell. The maximum stress in the tank body is 3.747MPa. So, based on this we get a safety factor of 5.33.

$$Factor\ of\ Safety = \frac{20}{3.747} = 5.33$$

24. Select **Bar von Mises stress** plot.

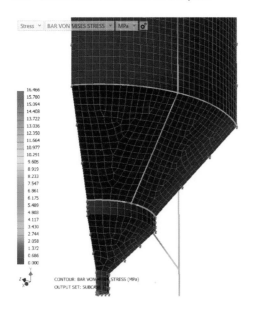

The maximum stress in the support structure is 16.466MPa. Based on this factor of safety is 16.7.

$$Factor\ of\ Safety = \frac{275}{16.466} = 16.7$$

Support structure meets the current design criteria.

25. Close File.

Fatigue – An Overview

"Fatigue is the weakening of a material caused by repeatedly applied loads. It is the progressive and localized structural damage that occurs when a material is subjected to cyclic loading. The nominal maximum stress values that cause such damage may be much less than the strength of the material typically quoted as the ultimate tensile stress limit, or the yield stress limit." (Wikipedia)

Engineering Background

Fatigue failure is the process in which a microscopic crack will grow when stresses vary due to time-varying loads, and when there is some tension in each cycle. As the crack grows with each cycle, the cross-sectional area supporting the load reduces to the point where the part fails catastrophically. Unlike a static failure, in which the part usually develops a large displacement because the stress exceeds the yield strength, a fatigue failure usually occurs without warning. It is sudden and total, and hence can be dangerous. Fatigue is a complicated phenomenon and is only partially understood. No analytical design approach provides precise results, in part because the phenomena is due to "random" factors in the material. Fatigue is one branch of engineering that requires material testing to guard against failure.

None-the-less you can benefit from a "starting point" to design the product before any testing is begun. Stress-Life and Strain-Life are the two basic analytical methods to determine fatigue life. Out of the two methods Stress-Life is most commonly used and will be focus of this chapter.

Stress-Life S-N Diagram

The stress-life method is characterized by the S-N curve, where S represents the alternating stress that causes failure, and N represents corresponding the number of cycles. A representative S-N curve for ferrous material, like Steel, is shown below.

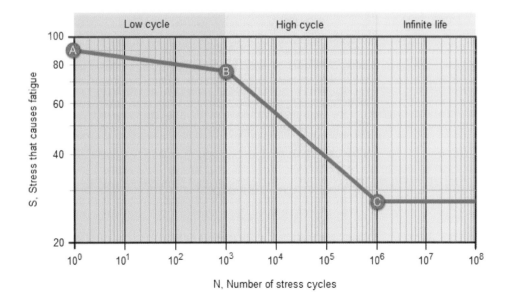

For Nonferrous materials the curve is not horizontal after point C as shown above.

CHAPTER 11
Fatigue – An Overview

The points on the curve correspond to these values:

A.   Ultimate tensile strength, S_{ut}. Failure occurs on 1 cycle.

B.   End of "low cycle" region, generally at 1000 cycles. The stress is some fraction of the tensile strength, $f \times S_{ut}$. The value f is generally between 0.9 and 0.78. (See below)

C.   End of "high cycle" region, generally at a point between 10^6 and 10^7 cycles. The corresponding stress is the endurance limit, S_e, at a specified number of cycles N_e.

Typically, a sample is loaded to a certain stress value, unloaded, and then loaded in the opposite direction. This is repeated until the part fails, which gives one point (N_1, S_1) on the S-N curve. The test is repeated with another specimen at a different level of stress until it fails, giving another point (N_2, S_2), and so on until the entire curve is created.

Fatigue Strength Fraction

The fatigue strength at the end of the low cycle region (point B) is set to $f \times S_{ut}$ where $f = 0.9$ by some sources while others used a complex calculation (and some assumptions) to create a value that depends on the ultimate strength. The result of such a calculation is shown below.

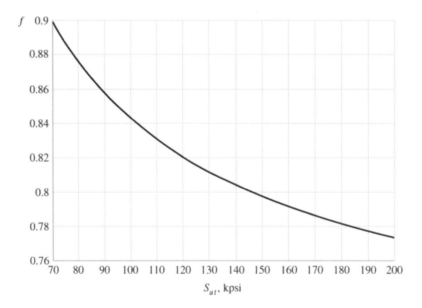

(Source obtained from Budynas, Richard G. and Nisbett, J. Keith, *Shigley's Mechanical Engineering Design*, McGraw-Hill, 9th Edition, 2011, Figure 6-18, page 285.)

Stress-Life Material behaviour

The S-N curve can be created for a real part or a test specimen, but most published data is for a rotating beam test specimen. The endurance limit S'_e found from such tests are applicable only to the test specimen. To use the data for actual parts, several factors need to be applied. The calculation of these factors is beyond the scope of this book. Please refer to a text book (such as Shigley's Mechanical Engineering Design) for details on applying the modifying factors.

$$S_e = k_a k_b k_c k_d k_e k_f S'_e$$

where

- S_e is the endurance limit for a specific part.

- S'_e is the endurance limit for a test specimen.

- k_a is a surface factor that accounts for the finish (ground, machined, forged, and so on).

- k_b is a size factor that accounts for the size of the part.

- k_c is a loading factor that accounts for different types of loading (bending, axial, torsion).

- k_d is a temperature factor.

- k_e is a reliability factor to account for scatter in the test results from one specimen to another.

- k_f is a miscellaneous factor to account for everything else (residual stress, directional characteristics, corrosion, electrolytic plating, and so on).

CHAPTER 11
Fatigue – An Overview

Fluctuating Stresses

The S-N curve generated for a rotating beam test specimen uses a fully reversing load; that is, the maximum and minimum stresses are the same magnitude but in tension and compression, as shown below.

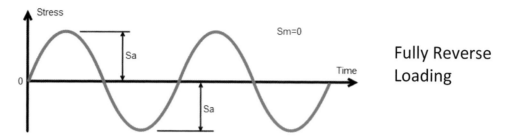

Fully Reverse Loading

If the load is not fully reversed, as shown below, the S-N curve would have different values.

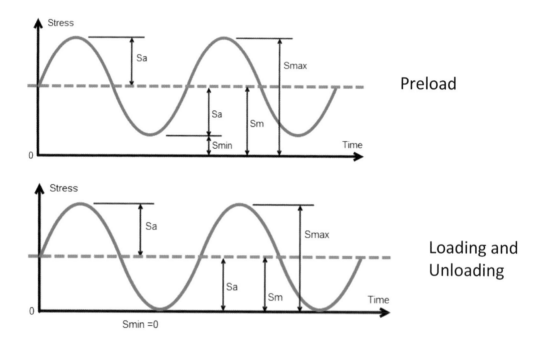

Preload

Loading and Unloading

Where:

S_{min} = minimum stress

S_{max} = maximum stress

S_a = alternating stress component = $\left|\dfrac{S_{max} - S_{min}}{2}\right|$

S_m = midrange (or mean) stress component = $\dfrac{S_{max} + S_{min}}{2}$

Instead of creating different S-N curves for different loadings, different theories are used to adjust the alternating stress for use in the S-N curve to find the life. The adjusted value is known as the zero-mean alternating stress, S_{a0}. Various fatigue criteria are available for the adjustment. These are generally shown on a graph such as below.

S_e = endurance strength

S_y = yield strength

S_{ut} = ultimate tensile strength

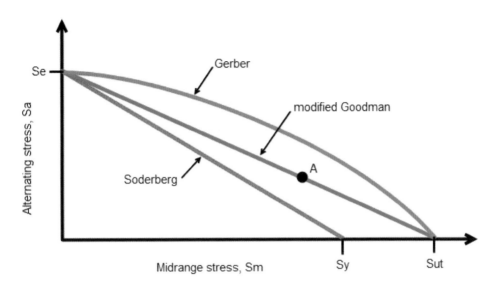

Any point "A" on the criteria is a fatigue strength for a given midrange value. If the alternating stress is below the line, the part has infinite life.

The equations for the different criteria are given in the table below. They are used to derive the adjustment to the alternating stress to calculate the zero-mean alternating stress, S_{a0}.

Fatigue Criteria	Equation for Line	Equation for Zero-mean Alternating Stress, S_{a0}
Modified Goodman	$\dfrac{S_a}{S_e} + \dfrac{S_m}{S_{ut}} = 1$	$S_{a0} = S_a \dfrac{1}{1 - S_m/S_{ut}}$
Soderberg	$\dfrac{S_a}{S_e} + \dfrac{S_m}{S_y} = 1$	$S_{a0} = S_a \dfrac{1}{1 - S_m/S_y}$
Gerber	$\dfrac{S_a}{S_e} + \left(\dfrac{S_m}{S_{ut}}\right)^2 = 1$	$S_{a0} = S_a \dfrac{1}{1 - \left(S_m/S_{ut}\right)^2}$

To re-iterate, the zero-mean alternating stress (S_{a0}) can be used on the S-N curve to determine the life of a part as shown below.

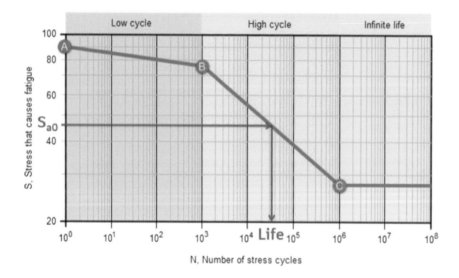

Fatigue Analysis within Inventor Nastran

The fatigue calculations are performed on solid, shell and line (both bar and beam) elements. Other element types can be included in the stress analysis (such as rigid elements), but the fatigue life will be ignored for these other element types. Because the fatigue calculation uses the method of superposition (which states the results due to multiple loads are the sum of the results due to each load), separation contact cannot be included in the analysis.

Below are the four steps required to carry out a fatigue analysis within Inventor Nastran.

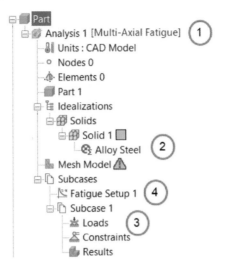

STEP 1 - Fatigue Analysis Types

Within Inventor Nastran you need to select the type of fatigue analysis you require. Currently you can either select Multi-Axial Fatigue or Vibration Fatigue. We will focus on the Multi-Axial Fatigue.

 Vibration fatigue analysis performs a random vibrations analysis ("Random Response"). The applied load is a power spectral density (PSD).

STEP 2 - Material Properties

The fatigue analysis can be performed using a stress-life calculation or a strain-life calculation. This selection is made within the Fatigue Setup (step 4 in the above steps). Each method uses different material input, but the fatigue material properties for each are entered by editing the material properties and clicking the "Fatigue" button.

Each material can have its own fatigue properties. In fact, it may be necessary to create additional materials to accurately represent the fatigue properties for each part. In a normal stress analysis, the material properties are approximately the same for a given class of material. For example, it does not matter whether you choose a "high strength steel" or a "low carbon steel" from the standpoint of the stress results. The modulus of elasticity and Poisson's Ratio for steel are generally the same for different chemistries within the same class of steel.

But the fatigue material properties include effects such as size of the part, heat treatment, and type of loading. Therefore, it is often necessary to use different materials for different parts just to be able to represent the fatigue material properties.

CHAPTER 11
Fatigue – An Overview

Stress-Life Material Properties

The material properties for a stress-life calculation defines the S-N curve and are represented by two points:

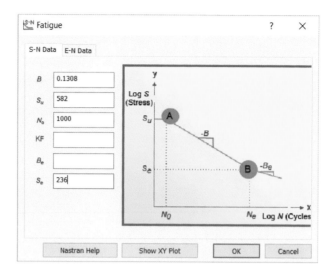

A. The point (N_0, S_u) represents the transition from low cycle to high cycle fatigue.

B. The point (N_e, S_e) represents the transition to infinite life. Ferrous material like steel have a well-defined endurance limit; that is, the S-N curve is horizontal after this point. Nonferrous metals and alloys do not have a true endurance limit but typically transition to a "more infinite life" at some number of cycles and level of stress.

- S_u is the stress at the transition from low cycle to high cycle (point A). This value is typically the ultimate tensile strength of the material, the yield strength or some fraction of those.

   o If the ultimate strength is used, then the life calculation follows the modified Goodman method.

   o If the yield strength is used, then the life calculation follows the Soderberg method.

   o The slope of the S-N curve is usually not flat in the low cycle region. Point A is usually some fraction of the ultimate strength. If the fraction of the ultimate strength is entered for Su, the slope of the S-N curve will be more accurate.

- N_0 is the number of cycles at the transition from low cycle to high cycle (point A). This value is typically 1000 cycles.

- S_e is the endurance strength at the transition to infinite life (point B). This input is not the value for the polished test specimen. This input is the fully corrected endurance limit based on the material, size, and other factors. That is, $S_e = k_a k_b k_c k_d k_e k_f S'_e$.

- N_e is the number of cycles at the transition to infinite life (point B). This is not input but is used to calculate the slope B.

- **B** is the slope of the S-N curve in the high cycle region; that is, from point A to point B. (Although the slope is negative, the software uses a positive input.) Since the S-N curve is a log-log plot, B is calculated as follows. Note that "log" is the base 10 logarithm; it is not the natural logarithm ("ln"). B is typically around 0.1 for steel.

$$B = \frac{\log(S_u) - \log(S_e)}{\log(N_e) - \log(N_0)}$$

- **B$_e$** is the slope of the S-N curve after the endurance limit; that is, at number of cycles higher than N$_e$.

- **KF** is a stress correction factor. If the mesh does not represent a particular stress concentration, this value could be used to correct the calculated stresses for the missing effect. However, note that this multiplier affects *all* nodes in the material.

A value of 1 is used in the event when the KF value field is not specified

STEP 3 - Load History
Fatigue is all about loads that vary over a cycle.

Multi-Axial Fatigue Loading
Since multi-axial fatigue analysis is a linear static stress analysis, the same types of loads applicable to linear stress can be applied to the fatigue analysis. Each load can be assigned to a load history to describe how it changes throughout the cycle.

Loads that are not assigned to a load history are constant over the cycle.

Time Value (X input)

The time used for the load history is significant because the calculated life is in units of time, not in units of cycles. See the description for the Event Duration in the next section.

Load Magnitude (Y input)

Inventor Nastran is looking for the peaks in the load history cycle. What happens in between the peaks is not relevant. For example, all three load histories represented below will produce identical results. Since the last representation is the easiest to enter, this is the type of input that will be used most often.

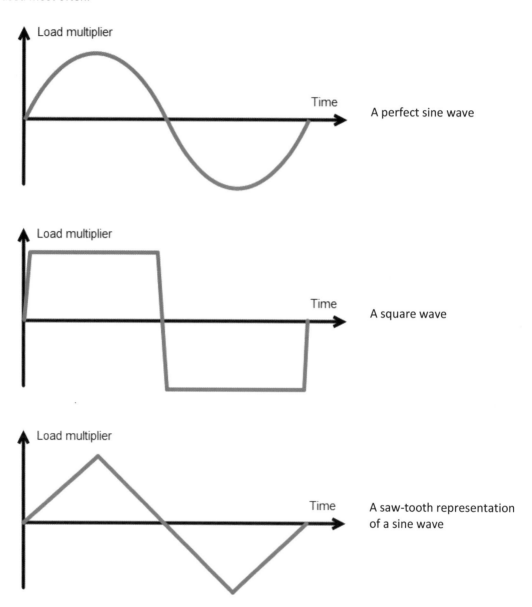

A perfect sine wave

A square wave

A saw-tooth representation of a sine wave

Identical load histories for reversing load

Each applied load creates a separate static analysis that is solved and then combined (per the load history) to create stress results used for the fatigue calculation. To reduce the analysis runtime, identical loads applied to different areas of the model should be applied using one load entry instead of multiple entries.

Vibration Fatigue Loading

The loading in a vibration fatigue analysis is a power spectral density (PSD). The setup is identical to a random response analysis.

Since the fatigue results are related to time, the Event Duration must be provided in the Fatigue Setup dialog).

STEP 4 - Additional Fatigue Setup

The Fatigue Setup dialog box is used to set the following items:

- **Approach** determines whether the calculations is based on the stress-life calculation (using the S-N data entered for the material properties) or strain-life calculation (using the E-N data entered for the material properties).

- **Method** determines whether Maximum principal, Von Mises or Maximum Shear stress (or strain) is to be used for the fatigue life calculations. All three methods combine the multi-axial stress state into a single, combined value.

- **Threshold.** This value is normally left blank.

- **Event Duration** is a way to specify that one cycle is longer than the time span indicated by the load histories. For example, an indexing machine may cycle once a minute, but the actual load cycle lasts only 5 seconds. The input for the load history would be for the 5 seconds duration, and the Event Duration would be the full 60 seconds.

   If left blank the value will be taken from the load curve definition.

- If the Event Duration is blank or shorter than the time span from the load histories, the value defaults to the longest time span from the load histories.

- **Time Conversion Factor** multiplies the Event Duration. It is typically used to convert the time from seconds to another unit of time. For example, to convert seconds to hours, the conversion factor would be 2.77E-4 (= 1 hr/3600 seconds).

$$Time\ for\ one\ cycle = Event\ Duration \times Time\ Conversion\ Factor$$

Results: Multi-Axial Fatigue

The multi-axis fatigue analysis produces the following results:

1. One set of static stress results is produced for each applied load: stress, displacement, and so on (see below). The results are based on the entered load and are not adjusted by the load history.

2. The Solid Life contour is the calculated time until failure at each node. This is not the number of cycles. To calculate the number of cycles to failure, divide the Life by the Event Duration.

3. The Solid Damage contour is 1/number of cycles to failure.

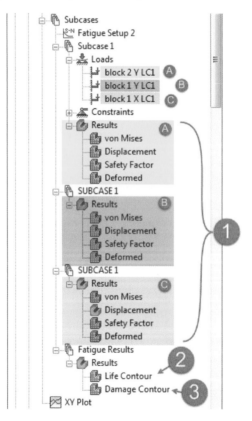

3 Load sets, 3 sets of results (not necessarily in the same order)

If the number of cycles to failure were to be calculated by hand, the following procedure would be used:

1.	If the calculated stress is compressive, the number of cycles to failure is assumed to be infinite.
2.	If the calculated stress is tensile, the maximum stress (S_{max}) and minimum stress (S_{min}) are determined from all of the points throughout the defined cycle.
3.	The midrange stress is calculated as follows: $$S_m = \frac{S_{max} + S_{min}}{2}$$
4.	The alternating stress is calculated as follows: $$S_a = \left| \frac{S_{max} - S_{min}}{2} \right|$$
5.	When the midrange stress is positive (tension), the alternating stress is adjusted to account for the non-zero mean stress. The zero-mean alternating stress is: $$S_{a0} = \frac{S_a}{1 - \dfrac{S_m}{S_u}}$$ If the mean stress is negative (compression), then $S_{a0}=S_a$.
6.	The S-N curve is interpolated using the zero-mean alternating stress to calculate the number of cycles: $$if\ K_f \times S_{a0} > S_e\ (finite\ life), N = N_0 \left(\frac{S_u}{K_f \times S_{a0}} \right)^{\frac{1}{B}}$$ $$if\ K_f S_{a0} \le S_e\ (infinite\ life), N = N_e \left(\frac{S_e}{K_f \times S_{a0}} \right)^{\frac{1}{B_e}}$$

7. If the load history consists of one "cycle", then the calculated life N in cycles is converted to time, based on the event duration for one cycle.

$$Life = N \times Event\ Duration$$

If the load history consists of multiple cycles at different stress levels, the Palmgren-Miner's rule and rain-flow counting is used to calculate the damage that occurs during one load history:

$$Damage = \sum \frac{n_i}{N_i}$$

where n_i is the number of cycles at a stress level of S_{ao} and N_i is the calculated number of cycles to failure at a stress level of S_{ao}. The life is then calculated as follows:

$$Life = \frac{Event\ Duration}{Damage}$$

The time correction factor, if entered by the user, is applied to the calculated life to convert the value to a different unit of time.

If the value entered for S_u is the ultimate tensile strength, then this procedure is equivalent to the modified Goodman relation:

$$\frac{S_a}{S_e} + \frac{S_m}{S_{ut}} = 1$$

If the value entered for S_u is the yield strength, then this procedure is equivalent to the Soderberg line:

$$\frac{S_a}{S_e} + \frac{S_m}{S_y} = 1$$

Below is a link to an AU Class on Fatigue presented by John Holtz on which most of the information in this chapter is based on.

https://www.autodesk.com/autodesk-university/class/Durability-101-Dont-get-tired-Fatigue-2016

Information in this chapter and the remaining chapters have also referenced information from the following book.

Shigley's Mechanical Engineering Design, McGraw-Hill, 9th Edition, from Budynas, Richard G. and Nisbett, J. Keith,

Rotating Shaft – Hand Calculation

(Source obtained from Budynas, Richard G. and Nisbett, J. Keith, <u>Shigley's Mechanical Engineering Design</u>, McGraw-Hill, 9th Edition, 2011, Example 6-9, pages 299-300)

A rotating steel shaft with the following properties is simply supported in ball bearings at A and D:

- Ultimate tensile strength S_{ut} = 690MPa

- f = 0.844 (fatigue strength fraction, for S at end of low cycle)

- Polished endurance limit S'_e = 345MPa

- Surface factor k_a = 0.798

- Size factor k_b = 0.858

- Stress concentration at shoulder B, K_t = 1.65 (referenced book uses 1.55)

- All fillets 3mm radius.

<u>Goal</u>: Estimate the life

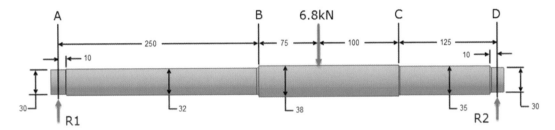

All dimensions in millimeters

<u>Solution:</u>

The transition from low cycle to high cycle is assumed to occur at 1000 cycles and S_u, is.

$$S_u = f \times S_{ut} = 0.844 \times 690 = 582 MPa$$

The transition from high cycle to infinite life is assumed to occur at 1E6 cycles and S_e. The corrected endurance limit S_e is calculated using the correction factors k_a through k_f (not to be confused with the stress concentration factor K_f), where k_c through k_f are assumed to be 1.

$$S_e = k_a k_b k_c k_d k_e k_f S'_e = 0.798 \times 0.858 \times 345 = 236 MPa$$

From a moment diagram, shaft diameters, and stress concentrations at each fillet, it can be shown that the maximum stress will occur at B where the moment M_B is 695.5 Nm. The section modulus is.

$$\frac{I}{c} = \frac{\pi d^3}{32} = \frac{\pi 32^3}{32} = 3.217 \times 10^3 \, mm^3 = 3.217 \times 10^{-6} \, m^3$$

and the stress is.

$$\sigma_B = K_t \frac{M_B}{I/c} = 1.65 \frac{695.5 \; Nm}{3.217 \times 10^{-6} \; m^3} = 356 \; MPa$$

Here we have used the K_t instead of K_f as we will be comparing results with Inventor Nastran which will be using precise geometry to represent notches fillets etc.

Because the stress reverses completely, the maximum and minimum stress are S_{max} = 356 MPa (tension) and S_{min} = –356 MPa (compression) leading to the mean and alternating stress of S_m = 0 and S_a = 356 MPa.

Since the mean stress is 0, the zero-mean alternating stress is S_{a0} = S_a = 356MPa.

The slope of the S-N curve is

$$B = \frac{\log(S_u) - \log(S_e)}{\log(N_e) - \log(N_0)} = \frac{\log(582) - \log(236)}{\log(1E6) - \log(1E3)} = 0.1308$$

Interpolating the S-N curve at the zero-mean alternating stress gives the answer

$$N = N_0 \left(\frac{S_u}{S_{a0}}\right)^{\frac{1}{B}} = 1000 \left(\frac{582}{356}\right)^{\frac{1}{0.1308}} = 42,855 \; cycles$$

DP10 – Fatigue Analysis – Rotating Shaft

Key features and workflows introduced in this design problem

	Key Features/Workflows
1	**Fixed Constraint**
2	**Edge Load**
3	**Rigid Body Connector**
4	**Multi-Axis Fatigue Analysis Setup**
5	**Load time based**
6	**Global and Local Mesh Control**
7	**Define S-N Curve**
8	**Fatigue Results**

Introduction

Although many products are satisfactory under the design loads compared to the material property such as the yield strength (with an appropriate factor of safety), they often fail because the product experiences thousands or millions of load cycles throughout their life. Such loads can cause a product to fail at a load magnitude that is much smaller than the load required to reach a material strength. Such failure is known as fatigue.

In this design problem we are going to analyse the shaft used in the previous fatigue hand calculation.

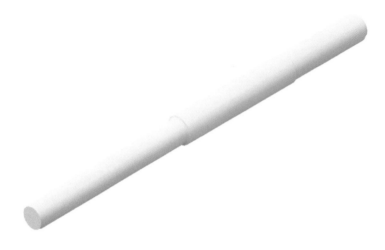

Design Information

Material - **AISI Carbon Steel 1050 Cold drawn**
Youngs Modulus - **200GPa**
Yield Limit - **480MPa**
Ultimate Tensile Strength- **690MPa**
f = **0.844**
S'_e = **345 MPa**
k_a = **0.798**
k_b = **0.858**

Design Goal

1. To compare results with hand calculations.

Workflow of Design Problem 10

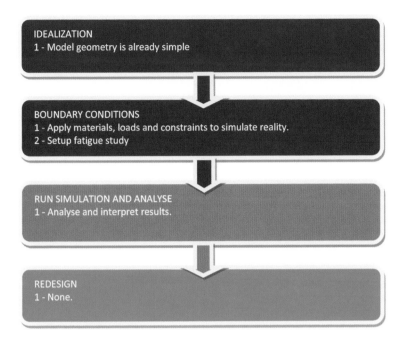

Idealization

The part file is already simple and therefore does not need to go through any further idealization.

1. Open *Shaft.ipt*

Boundary conditions

2. Select **Environments** tab > Select **Autodesk Inventor Nastran.**

3. **Right Click** Analysis 1 > Select **Edit** > For Type select **Multi-Axial Fatigue**

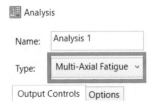

4. Click **OK** > Right Click **Generic** material > Select Edit > Select **Materials** > Select **AISI Carbon Steel 1050 Cold drawn** from the Inventor Nastran materials library > Specify **690** for S_T > Specify **480** for S_Y > Select **Fatigue** from Analysis Specific Data.

5. Specify **0.1308** for B > Specify **582** for S_u > Specify **1000** for N_o > Specify **236** for S_e

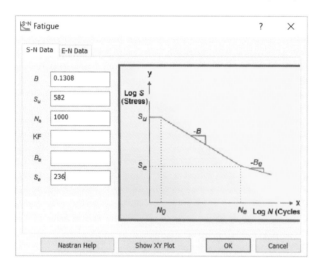

Not specifying a value for B_e will maintain the value of S_e, beyond point N_e. For Ferrous materials this assumption is valid.

Normally you will not need to specify KF if your CAD model contains geometrical details like notches, fillets, holes etc.

S'_e are typically half of S_u for steel components. For iron, aluminium and copper alloys, S'_e is typically 0.4 times the ultimate tensile strength.

6. Click **OK** twice > Select **Connectors** from the Prepare panel > Select **Rigid Body** from Connector Type > Select end face of shaft as shown below.

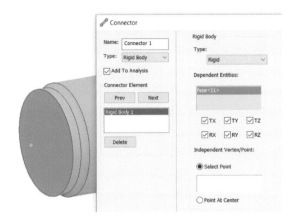

7. Click in the Select Point selection box > Select **Work point <1>** for Independent Vertex/Point > Adjust display options as desired.

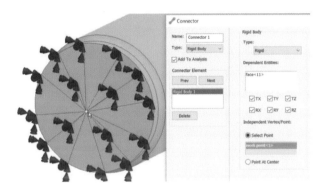

8. Click **Next** > Add another rigid body connector on the other side of the shaft > Click **OK**.

9. Select **Constraints** > Select w**ork point <1>** as shown > Select the **work point <2>** on the other side of the shaft > Unselect **Ry** and **Rz** degrees of freedom.

CHAPTER 12

DP10 – Fatigue Analysis – Rotating Shaft

10. Click **OK** > Select **Loads** > Select edge as shown below > Specify -6800 for Magnitude in Fy field > Select **Define New Table** icon.

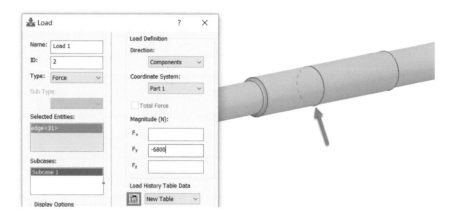

💡 Use split command to split faces to help generate edges and faces to apply loads.

11. Select **Load Scale Factor vs Time** for Type > Specify the values as shown below.

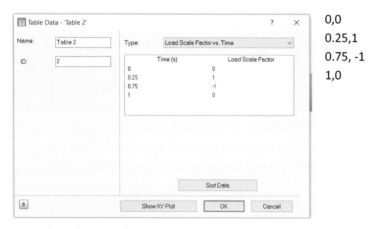

0,0
0.25,1
0.75, -1
1,0

12. Select **Show XY Plot**

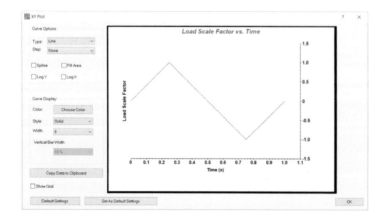

13. Click **OK** three times > Select **Mesh Control** > Select Face Data option by clicking in the Selected Faces box > Specify **0.5** for Element Size (mm) > Select all four fillets on the shaft

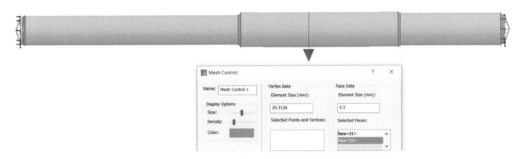

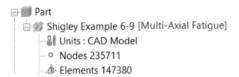

14. Click **OK** > Select **Mesh Settings** > Specify **5** for Element Size (mm) > Select **Settings** > Specify **1.2** for Max Element Growth Rate > Select Project Midside Nodes > Click **OK** twice.

```
☐─🔲 Part
   └─🔷 Shigley Example 6-9 [Multi-Axial Fatigue]
        ├─🌡 Units : CAD Model
        ├─○ Nodes 235711
        └─🔷 Elements 147380
```

147,380 elements will be generated.

15. Click **OK** > **Right Click** Fatigue Set 1 > Select **Edit** > Select **von Mises** for Method.

🖊 Fatigue life will be based on Von Mises stress

16. Click **OK.**

CHAPTER 12
DP10 – Fatigue Analysis – Rotating Shaft

Run simulation and analyse

17. Select **Run** > Click **OK** once run is complete.

18. Select **von Mises** stress plot > Unselect **Deformed** from the Results panel > Select **Object Visibility** > Unselect **Loads** > Unselect **Constraints** > Unselect **Connectors** > Unselect **Mesh Controls**.

Maximum Von Mises stress is 354MPa.

19. Select **Displacement** plot

Maximum displacement is 1.498mm

20. Select **Life Contour**.

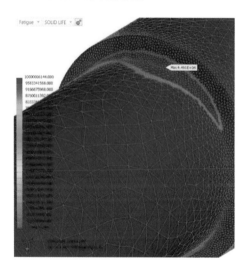

Minimum Life is 44,912 this is within 5% of the calculated value. This percentage difference is acceptable.

It is also worth noting that the Nastran results are more accurate as the hand calculation is only based on bending stress calculation. Inventor Nastran includes all stresses including shear stress in addition to having detailed geometry and thus being less reliant on stress concentration factors. Stress concentration factors can have a significant impact on the life of the product.

21. Close File.

DP11 – Fatigue Analysis – Connecting Rod

Key features and workflows introduced in this design problem

	Key Features/Workflows
1	**Fixed Constraint**
2	**Bearing Load**
3	**Multi-Axis Fatigue Analysis Setup**
4	**Load time based**
5	**Define S-N Curve with supporting information**
6	**Fatigue Results**

CHAPTER 13
DP11 – Fatigue Analysis – Connecting Rod

Introduction

Fatigue failures are frequently observed in various components of piston engines. The reasons for such failures can be improper material selection, improper design, misalignment, improper lubrication etc. In this design problem we are going to determine the fatigue life of a connecting rod as shown below.

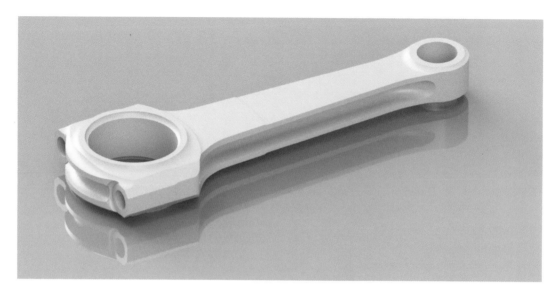

Design Information

Material - **AISI 1015 Hot Rolled**
Ultimate Tensile Strength – **340MPa**
Yield Limit - **190MPa**
Axial load - **15000N** (fully reversible load).

Design Goal

1. To determine fatigue life.
2. Fatigue life > 1E6

Workflow of Design Problem 11

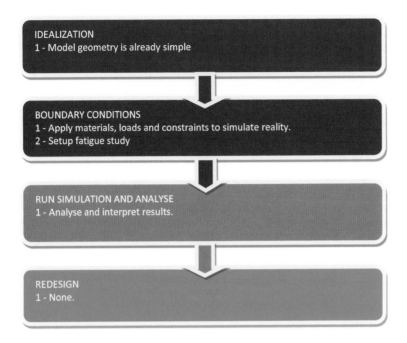

IDEALIZATION
1 - Model geometry is already simple

BOUNDARY CONDITIONS
1 - Apply materials, loads and constraints to simulate reality.
2 - Setup fatigue study

RUN SIMULATION AND ANALYSE
1 - Analyse and interpret results.

REDESIGN
1 - None.

Idealization

The part file is already simple and therefore does not need to go through any further idealization.

1.   Open *Shaft.ipt*

Boundary conditions

2.   Select **Environments** tab > Select **Autodesk Inventor Nastran.**

3.   **Right Click** Analysis 1 > Select **Edit** > For Type select **Multi-Axial Fatigue**

4. Click **OK** > Right Click **Steel, Mild** material > Select **Edit** > Select **Materials** > Select **AISI Carbon Steel 1015 Hot Rolled** from the Inventor Nastran materials library > Specify **340** for S_T > Specify **190** for S_Y.

Tensile (UTS) and Yield strength values can be easily obtained from various sources including matweb.com

5. Select **Fatigue** from Analysis Specific Data.

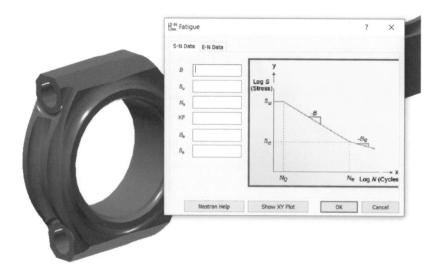

For ferrous materials, like steel here, you only need to specify the following values

B – Gradient of the curve in the high cycle region.

S_u – UTS value of material.

N_o – In most cases is always sets to 1000.

S_e – Endurance limit.

To determine B we first need to find the endurance limit. As mentioned earlier data is only available for test specimens and is usually denoted as S'_e. For most steel components we can assume the test specimen endurance limit is[1].

$$S'_e = 0.5 S_u \qquad \text{Equation 1}$$

$$S'_e = 0.5 \times 340 = 170$$

To determine actual endurance limit S_e we need to take account of the following factors[2].

$$S_e = k_a k_b k_c k_d k_e k_f S'_e \qquad \text{Equation 2}$$

where

- S_e is the endurance limit for a specific part.

- S'_e is the endurance limit for a test specimen.

- k_a is a surface factor that accounts for the finish (ground, machined, forged, and so on).

- k_b is a size factor that accounts for the size of the part.

- k_c is a loading factor that accounts for different types of loading (bending, axial, torsion).

- k_d is a temperature factor.

- k_e is a reliability factor to account for scatter in the test results from one specimen to another.

- k_f is a miscellaneous factor to account for everything else (residual stress, directional characteristics, corrosion, electrolytic plating, and so on).

In this design problem we are going to assume 1 for all factors except the following.

$$Ka = aS_u^b \qquad \text{Equation 3}$$

Where[3]

Surface Finish	Factor a (MPa)	Exponent b
Ground	1.58	-0.085
Machined or cold-drawn	4.51	-0.265
Hot-rolled	57.7	-0.718
As-forged	272	-0.995

And as we are using axial load[4]

$$Kc = 0.85 \qquad \text{Equation 4}$$

So, using Equation 3 and above values for machined surface, we can calculate Ka.

$Ka = aS_u^b$ => $4.51 \times 340^{-0.265}$ => $4.51 \times 0.2134 = 0.962$

So, using equation 2 we can now determine S_e.

$S_e = 0.962 \times 0.85 \times 170 = 139$MPa.

CHAPTER 13
DP11 – Fatigue Analysis – Connecting Rod

It also important to note the value of actual S_u at 1000 cycles will be reduced by some factor as illustrated below.

$$S_f = f \times S_u \qquad \text{Equation 5}$$

Where.

f is fatigue strength fraction.

S_f is tensile strength at 1000 cycles.

For components with a Tensile Strength value (UTS) of 482MPa and below we can use 0.9 for f as illustrated below[5].

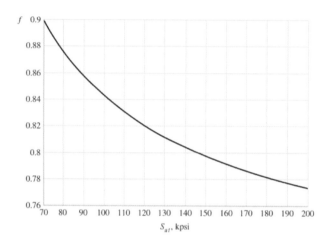

Where

70 kpsi = 482MPa & 200kpsi = 1379MPa

 If S_u value is between 70 and 200kpsi then you can take appropriate f value from the above.

As our material yield value of 340MPa is below 482MPa we can use a value of 0.9 for fatigue strength fraction to calculate Tensile Strength at 1000 cycles.

$$S_f = f \times S_u \qquad => 0.9 \times 340 = 306MPa$$

References.

1. (Source obtained from Budynas, Richard G. and Nisbett, J. Keith, *Shigley's Mechanical Engineering Design*, McGraw-Hill, 9th Edition, 2011, Section 6-7, page 282)
2. (Source obtained from Budynas, Richard G. and Nisbett, J. Keith, *Shigley's Mechanical Engineering Design*, McGraw-Hill, 9th Edition, 2011, Section 6-9, page 287)
3. (Source obtained from Budynas, Richard G. and Nisbett, J. Keith, *Shigley's Mechanical Engineering Design*, McGraw-Hill, 9th Edition, 2011, Table 6-2, page 288)
4. (Source obtained from Budynas, Richard G. and Nisbett, J. Keith, *Shigley's Mechanical Engineering Design*, McGraw-Hill, 9th Edition, 2011, Equation 6-26, page 290)
5. (Source obtained from Budynas, Richard G. and Nisbett, J. Keith, *Shigley's Mechanical Engineering Design*, McGraw-Hill, 9th Edition, 2011, Figure 6-18, page 285)

We now have the following values.

$S_u - 306MPa$

$N_o - 1000.$

$S_e - 139MPa.$

We now have all the information required to calculate B from the following equation.

The slope of the S-N curve is

$$B = \frac{\log(S_u) - \log(S_e)}{\log(N_e) - \log(N_0)}$$

Where Ne is usually 1 million cycles.

$$B = \frac{\log(306) - \log(139)}{\log(1E6) - \log(1E3)}$$

$$B = \frac{2.486 - 2.143}{6 - 3}$$

$$B = \frac{0.343}{3} = 0.114$$

6.   Specify **0.114** for B > Specify **306** for S_u > Specify **1000** for N_o > Specify **139** for S_e

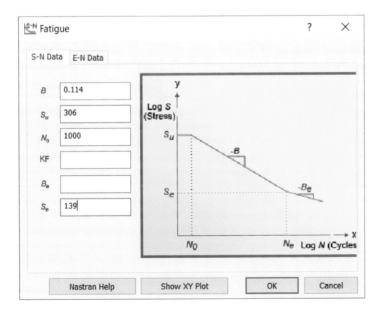

CHAPTER 13

7. Click **OK** twice > Select **Constraints** > Specify **Fixed** for Name > Select highlighted cylindrical face as shown.

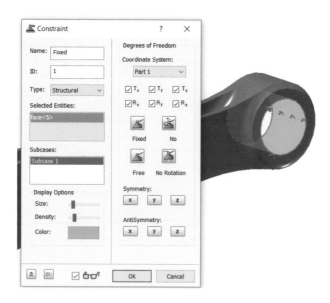

8. Click **OK** > Select **Loads** > Specify **Bearing Load** for Name > Select **Bearing Load** for Load Type > Select highlighted cylindrical face to apply load > Select **Components** for Direction > Specify **20000** for Magnitude in Fz field > Select Preview to adjust display options as desired.

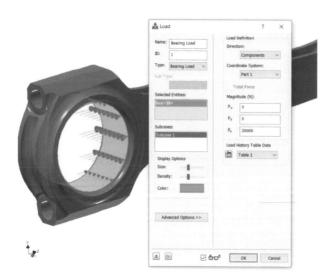

9. Select **Load Scale Factor vs Time** for Type > Specify the values as shown below

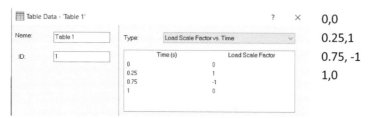

0,0

0.25,1

0.75, -1

1,0

10. Click **OK** twice > Select **Mesh Settings** > Specify **2** for Element Size (mm) > Select **Settings** > Specify **1.2** for Max Element Growth Rate > **Select** Project Midside Nodes > Click **OK** twice.

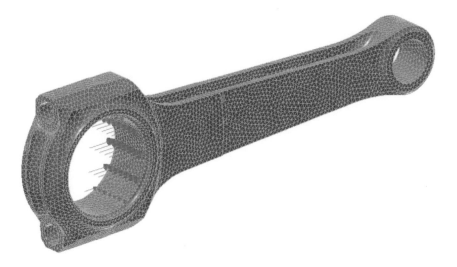

62,231 elements will be generated.

11. Click **OK** > **Right Click** Fatigue Set 1 > Select **Edit** > Select **von Mises** for Method.

12. Click **OK**.

Run simulation and analyse

13. Select **Run** > Click **OK** once run is complete.

14. Select **von Mises** stress plot > Unselect **Deformed** from the Results panel > Select **Object Visibility** > Unselect **Loads** > Unselect **Constraints**.

Maximum Von Mises stress is 166.5MPa.

15. Select **Displacement** from the results navigation bar.

Maximum displacement is 0.068mm.

16. Double Click **Life Contour** in the browser.

Minimum Life is 208,684.

This current design is not suitable under the current loading condition as it does not have an infinite life (1E6) and thus requires modifications to be acceptable.

17. Close File.